Wildlife in Alaska

WILDLIFE IN ALASKA

AN ECOLOGICAL RECONNAISSANCE

By

A. STARKER LEOPOLD

ASSOCIATE PROFESSOR OF ZOOLOGY, MUSEUM OF
VERTEBRATE ZOOLOGY, UNIVERSITY OF CALIFORNIA, BERKELEY

and

F. FRASER DARLING

SENIOR LECTURER IN ECOLOGY AND CONSERVATION,
UNIVERSITY OF EDINBURGH

Sponsored by
The New York Zoological Society and
ⓒ *The Conservation Foundation* 1953

GP

GREENWOOD PRESS, PUBLISHERS
WESTPORT, CONNECTICUT

reprint 1972

The Library of Congress has catalogued this publication as follows:

Library of Congress Cataloging in Publication Data

Leopold, Aldo Starker, 1913-
  Wildlife in Alaska.

    Bibliography: p.
    1. Wildlife conservation--Alaska. 2. Game and
game-birds--Alaska. 3. Natural resources--Alaska.
4. Wildlife management--Alaska. I. Darling, Sir
Frank Fraser, 1903-   joint author. II. Title.
S964.U6L46 1972   639'.9'09798   72-6927
ISBN 0-8371-6509-1

Originally published in 1953
by The Ronald Press Company, New York

Reprinted with the permission
of The Conservation Foundation, Inc.

First Greenwood Reprinting 1972

Library of Congress Catalogue Card Number 72-6927

ISBN 0-8371-6509-1

Printed in the United States of America

THE CONSERVATION FOUNDATION

is an independent organization established
to conduct research and to educate. Its
work is devoted to the conservation of the
earth's renewable resources.

FOREWORD

THIS FIELD STUDY concerns the great horned animals of Alaska and their environment in one of the last frontier lands of the world. A work of keen observation and scholarship, it analyzes the ever changing relationships between man, these grazing animals, and their habitats. It stresses the importance of wildlife management in a territory whose invaluable assets are the living natural resources on the land and in the adjacent waters.

With the development of Alaska's economy in mind, the authors recommend a broader and a more coordinated approach to the management of these resources. The adoption of such recommendations is particularly important in a region where the resources of the land, despite some early despoliation, are still largely intact and remain, with a few exceptions, the property of all the people of the United States. The situation presents a unique opportunity to initiate a comprehensive conservation program *before* the territory is subjected to haphazard development.

One of the recommendations made by the authors—and

one that will surely be endorsed by conservationists, natural scientists, and sportsmen everywhere—is that a number of unspoiled regions within Alaska be designated as wilderness areas before it is too late. An Arctic Wilderness Area, for example, should be set aside in the Brooks Range of northern Alaska, to protect an adequate reserve in that wonderful primitive region for posterity. Such action would provide, among other things, a field laboratory for long-range scientific studies of ecological relationships in the Arctic of North America.

We could not have been more fortunate in the selection of the reconnaissance team for this study. Two eminent naturalists, one from the Old World and one from the New, have pooled their knowledge and experience to produce this report. On behalf of the two sponsoring organizations, it is a deep pleasure to commend and to thank Dr. A. Starker Leopold and Dr. F. Fraser Darling for their accomplishment.

FAIRFIELD OSBORN
New York Zoological Society
The Conservation Foundation

New York, N. Y.
September, 1953

CONTENTS

MAPS

WILDLIFE IN ALASKA

1

THE TASK AND
THE ITINERARY

OUR JOURNEYS of observation have taken us over many thousands of miles of the Territory of Alaska. Our impression is of the grandeur and magnificence of this vast terrain, and yet of its newness in biological development and of tenderness as a habitat suffering the arrival and increase of western, civilized, technological man. Is he going to be the despoiler or the good steward of this last frontier?

In recording our impressions of a summer's travel and observation, we have dealt particularly with the status of caribou, moose, and reindeer and upon their future place in Alaskan economy and ecology. Perhaps even this limited segment of Alaska's conservation problem was more than we could fully assimilate in so short a period. But being in the position of outsiders, looking in upon new and fascinating ecologic situations and upon existing government programs designed to cope with them, we could perhaps bring to bear an objectivity of analysis that is denied the government employee who is surrounded by an aura of existing policies, programs, and commitments. That at least is our hope in presenting the thoughts that appear in these pages.

Our task, as greenhorns spending four months in 586,000 square miles of territory, has not been to attempt to solve the problems of conservation in Alaska, but to make an objective appraisal of them. We have tried to evaluate the potential importance of the ungulate mammals in the future economy of Alaska and set their conservation and management against those other forms of land use which might loom paramount, such as pastoralism, forestry, or agriculture. We have tried to remember the several values of big game for recreation, esthetic appreciation, and tourist attraction, and last but not least for food. The animals exist, also, in their own right and we should acknowledge this as part of the national responsibility. We have been particularly concerned with the place of the big game species in the economy of the native peoples of Alaska and have therefore had to consider some of the sociological problems of Eskimos and Indians. An attempt has been made to define the broad ecologic problems and the more specific planning which will be necessary in the future.

Our work consisted mainly of observation and interview and we wish to acknowledge the help we received in such generous fashion. The Fish and Wildlife Service, both in Washington and in Alaska, gave us every possible facility, including much transport in the field, which enabled us to get to remote places it would not have been possible for us to reach otherwise. Personally, they gave us a memorable companionship. We also have to thank the following organizations for their most friendly cooperation: The U. S. Public Health Service, Anchorage; the National Park Service; the Alaska Native Service; the Alaska Field Committee of the Department of Interior; and the University of Alaska. The Office of Naval Research gave us the hospitality of that unique institution, the Arctic Research Laboratory, at Point Barrow, and we wish to thank the director and ONR for the intellectual stimulation we received as well as for the hospitality of the laboratory.

*   *   *

Our itinerary was as follows: After arrival in Juneau, on June 1, 1952, we had the good fortune to fly to Chichagof Island and return by the Fish and Wildlife patrol ship *Grizzly Bear*. This trip enabled us to see something of the virgin Sitka spruce and hemlock forests of southeastern Alaska and of the black-tailed deer situation on the hilly forested islands where winter range is restricted to a narrow coastal strip measurable in yards. We flew to Anchorage where several agencies have bases and were privileged to walk a trapline operated by the Fish and Wildlife Service Predator Control Division in the Eagle River valley. The railroad was taken to Mt. McKinley National Park where we were fortunate enough to take part in the Dall sheep counts in the park area and to see something of the magnificent array of wild game which has sanctuary there. On returning to Anchorage we flew to Bethel on the Kuskokwim River; then by Fish and Wildlife Service airplane to near the mouth of the Kashunuk River, south of Hooper Bay, in the great area of lakes and low tundra used as a breeding ground by large numbers of various species of waterfowl. Our camp was never quiet, night or day, for the sound of black brant, emperor, white-fronted and cackling geese, of sandhill cranes and of myriads of sandpipers, plovers and phalaropes. We flew to Nunivak Island, taking part in the

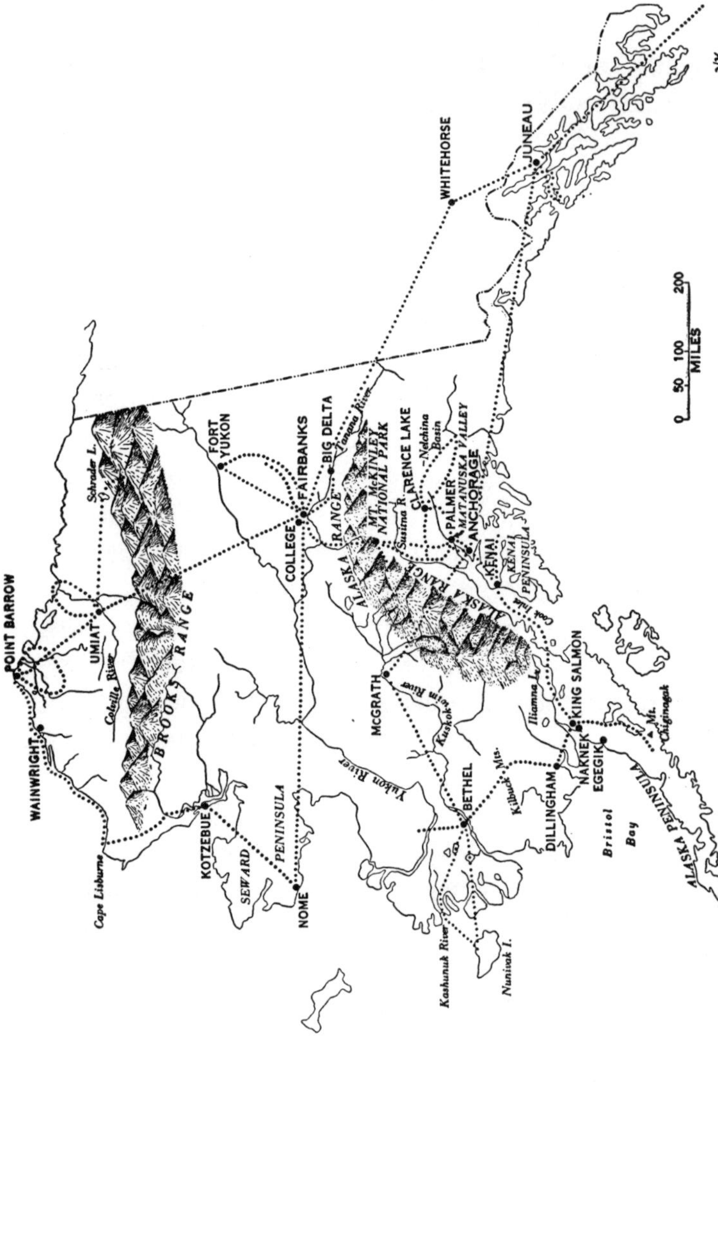

FIGURE 1. The itinerary of the authors during the period of field work in Alaska, June 1 to September 29, 1952.

muskox count and seeing that oft-described behavior of these animals in rapidly forming a defensive ring, calves to the center. Our stay there enabled us to examine the range situation in relation to past and present reindeer pastoralism, and we inspected the up-to-date system for corralling, slaughtering, processing and freezing installed by the Alaska Native Service. We returned to Bethel following a route south of Nelson Island and Baird Inlet, then across the Kilbuck Mountains to the Tikchik Lakes, turning due south to Dillingham and flying over a large forest fire on the way. In crossing from there to King Salmon we saw the fleet of boats in Kvichak Bay on the first day of the Bristol Bay salmon season. We were told later that the 1,000 boats were trailing 87 miles of drift nets. King Salmon is an important point in the Fish and Wildlife Service's administrative network of the salmon fishery and in the course of a few days we were able to realize something of the delicacy of the problems and the onerous duties of the administrative staff. Our travel down the Alaska Peninsula did not extend beyond Mother Goose Lake, west of Mount Chiginagak, but this allowed us to examine the wintering grounds of the herd of caribou resident on the peninsula and the area formerly occupied by reindeer herds around Egegik and Naknek. We were surprised by the richness of vegetation resulting from the volcanic origin of the soil.

We flew to Kenai via Iliamna Lake and up Cook Inlet, getting superb views of Iliamna Volcano and its glaciers, then flying along the bird cliffs of Chisik Island, which is a National Wildlife Refuge. Then by air and road we quartered much of the Kenai Peninsula, examining moose ranges and the influences of man in this relatively closely settled area.

On return to Anchorage we journeyed by road into the Susitna and Matanuska moose country where the rich broad-leaved shrub growth has favored a high density of moose. We flew then around the Talkeetna Mountains and into the Nelchina Basin where a herd of caribou is more or less resident and has recently increased as a result of protection from predators and from overhunting. We flew over the summer grounds where the animals were, over winter grounds where the results of their lichen hunting were plain to see, and over burned areas where caribou no longer visit.

We entrained to Fairbanks to fly to the Arctic Research Laboratory at Point Barrow, and from there flew over some of the coastal tundra, noting how the snowy owls were concentrated along the coast of the Arctic Ocean rather than being generally distributed. From Umiat, southeast of Barrow, we were able to see the interesting Cretaceous "downland" country along the Colville River. These low, rolling hills diminish northward into the coastal tundra of the Colville delta, and in a flight west from there as far as Teshekpuk Lake we saw herds of caribou bulls standing belly-deep in the shallows of the Arctic Ocean to escape mosquitoes. In association with two members of the National Park Service, we embarked on a rather ambitious program of examining parts of the spectacular Romanzof Mountains at the east end of the Brooks Range and were encamped for a week at the neck of Lake Schrader and Lake Peters. We missed a great movement of caribou by five days, but we had illuminating opportunities in exploring this very rough country after such a passage of animals. The ground still carried their scent. Our attempts to cross the Brooks Range by airplane up the Hulahula

River were unsuccessful, though the National Park personnel got through later with a lightened load.

At Fort Yukon we examined part of last season's catch of pelts of muskrat, marten, fox, lynx, beaver, and wolf. The trading posts in this Indian village collect a great many of the skins from the whole Yukon drainage extending back into Canada. Then we flew up the Yukon, being struck anew with the dynamic quality of a great river and its ecological influence in setting back succession by erosion and deposition, making for much plant colonization and new willow growth. A journey up the Steese Highway was made to see the types of burned-over woodland, of spruce "taiga" near the tree line, and of the open hills of rounded contour rising to approximately 5,000 feet. All this country is used by the remnants of the former vast Yukon-Tanana herd of caribou. We also visited Big Delta to see the bison range. It does not seem likely that the herd can increase or spread since there is little suitable habitat for bison in Alaska.

The west coast from Nome northward was visited in order to see the former reindeer ranges and the remnants of the great herds which reached their peak number in the 1930's. We were impressed by the changes in the herbage complex which have taken place in half a century. Our stay at Kotzebue was the more interesting because it is in effect the Eskimo capital of Alaska, a meeting place where slight differences in culture and techniques can be observed and where the Eskimos' beautiful dancing can be enjoyed. One of us was so fortunate as to make the coastal flight as far as the limestone cliffs of Cape Lisburne and on to Wainwright, one of the happiest and simplest, surely, of Alaskan Eskimo villages.

We were privileged for some time to enjoy the academic hospitality of the University of Alaska at College, Fairbanks. The physical setting of this institution must surely be unrivaled, looking over the gently undulating forested interior plain to high mountains culminating in Mount McKinley, 158 miles away. We felt that the intellectual ferment in this young institution matched its setting.

Our mission terminated in attending the Alaska Science Conference at McKinley National Park from September 22 to 27, 1952. One could not leave Alaska from such a gathering without being impressed by the large amount of research which is being done in the Territory and with what vigor the men and women of Alaska are determined that the spirit of science shall prevail.

2

THE OPPORTUNITY FOR WILDLIFE CONSERVATION IN ALASKA

A POLICY of wildlife conservation ideally should precede the penetration and development of any country new to civilized man. We know that in practice no new country has been developed with conservation in mind. Recognition of the need for conservation ordinarily comes when the native stocks of animals, which seemed limitless, are reduced to a point below the level of further economic exploitation or are threatened with actual extinction. Then people readily become conservation-minded. As a rule, the longer the period of exploitation, the more difficult of solution are the conservation problems.

Alaska is one of the new countries of the world and it is the last frontier of the United States. Its early development followed the familiar pattern of exploitation. The Russians depleted the stock of sea otters almost to extinction. Russians, Americans, Britons, and Japanese almost finished the fur seal herds of the Pribilof Islands. The caribou of southern and western Alaska disappeared, and so did the muskox of the north. A century of interference with the mammals of the western seas and coasts of Alaska so disorganized the hunting-food-gathering culture of the coastal Eskimos that for a time these people themselves were in grave danger of extinction. The salmon-packing industry, which blossomed into Alaska's most lucrative business, threatened to wipe out the prodigious runs.

When at last the concept of conservation emerged, and government bureaus undertook to rectify the carnage, most effort was directed toward protecting remaining breeding stocks from further exploitative use. At that time, with the disappearance of the bison and the passenger pigeon still fresh in mind, "stop the killing" seemed the immediate technique of conservation. An elaborate legal and administrative program was developed whose basic tenet was curbing excessive use of animal resources. Its application brought rapid and even spectacular increases in some species, slow and spotty increases in others; some did not respond.

In general, oceanic forms showed the most consistent response to protection. The recovery of the stocks of fur seal has been one of the shining successes of conservation in action, and the period of increase has been one of constant research in management of the stock as a continuing resource. The sea otter has not yet recovered, but research is being done and the species is increasing. Whales, walrus, and seals are at least holding their ground, and salmon, though still overfished, are being preserved at a reasonably safe level of abundance.

But among the animals of the land, results of a program based largely on protection from direct kill have been less uniformly satisfactory. Some species, like moose and black-tailed deer, have increased; others have continued to lose ground, as for example the caribou. Even protection from natural predators, in addition to protection from man, has not brought the desired response. The answer lies apparently in subtle changes in vegetation which accompanied the era of exploitation and which may affect the status of wild species even more drastically than direct killing. Whereas the ocean, as an environment for animals, is scarcely subject to alteration by man, the land is very subject indeed, and few are the remaining spots on earth that have not in some way been changed. Conservation and management of land mammals, therefore, must take into account habitat variables which, as far as we know, can be considered "constants" among oceanic species.

Yet, because Alaska is so newly occupied and so slightly altered, there is time for policies of conservation to be conceived, considered, and put in hand before really severe or irreversible devastation takes place. The lamentable state of the caribou, when it is completely understood, may be correctable. The muskox can perhaps be restored to the Arctic prairie. Much of northern Alaska, in point of fact, has scarcely been altered. There are vast expanses where the fauna and flora are essentially virgin. In short, a rare opportunity is presented to predetermine the course of development and utilization of wildlife resources in an area that is still not far removed from original condition.

3

WILDLIFE IN RELATION TO
OTHER RESOURCES

THE SIGNIFICANCE of wildlife resources in the economy of Alaska remains very high even today when the technologies of food preparation and of logistics have removed them from being a paramount or crucial factor in the survival of the human population. Historically, there are innumerable examples of wild game being the bridge over which spreading cultures have crossed from uncertainty to sure establishment in new terrain. One of the earliest Anglo-Saxon land charters which has survived lists the wildlife habitats such as bird marshes as being equally valuable with the cleared agricultural ground. Nevertheless, as agricultural, pastoral, and industrial development continues, wildlife resources tend to become less valued and may even become inimical to the new land use. How is it then that in Alaska, wildlife and fisheries have continued to dominate the economic scene despite material progress in the development of mining, timber mills, agriculture, and, more recently, industry? What will be the *future* place of wildlife as Alaskan economy matures? Will it retain its present importance?

In an attempt to prognosticate the answers to these and other questions regarding Alaskan economy, the Alaska Field Committee of the Department of Interior has prepared two recent reports (1951 and 1952), the first of which includes a table of anticipated incomes a decade hence, reproduced here as Table 1.

TABLE 1. Anticipated sources of income in Alaska in 1962, as listed in the 1951 report of the Alaska Field Committee, Department of Interior (K. J. Kadow, ed.)

Fisheries and wildlife	$150,000,000
Civilian government expenditures	125,000,000
Military expenditures	100,000,000
Tourist and related industries	100,000,000
Forest products and related industries	60,000,000
Electro-metallurgical and other mineral industries	60,000,000
Miscellaneous, including agriculture	25,000,000
	$620,000,000

These figures were arrived at on the basis of a series of questionable assumptions, such as a population of 300,000 in place of the present 129,000 and the continuing defense spending, which may go up or down with changes in international relations. But it is highly significant that fishery and wildlife products are still shown at the top of the list of income sources. Likewise the anticipated growing importance of the tourist industry is in considerable degree linked to the opportunity for hunting and fishing and for seeing the larger animals in parks and along the highways. Thus it seems to us that we can safely assume that wildlife resources will occupy a continued place of dominance in Alaskan economy.

Nor is the full value of Alaskan wildlife measured in dollars and cents. Game and fish as a source of food, and among native peoples as a source of clothing, is still very important. Because of the unfavorable climate for agriculture and livestock husbandry, production of wild animals for meat and hides will continue to be of great significance to Alaskans.

We attempt here to weigh the present and probable future values of all the principal natural resources of Alaska and to justify the foregoing contention that wildlife and fisheries are in fact the most valuable resources of the Territory and as such deserve the most careful husbandry.

Cash value of wildlife products

The fishery is Alaska's most valuable resource in terms of past and present exploitation, with salmon contributing the bulk of the catch. Table 2 summarizes the annual value of the recent take of fish products from Territorial waters.

TABLE 2. Approximate current value of the fishery products packed in Alaska. (Fish and Wildlife Service data)

Salmon	$100,000,000
Herring products	6,500,000
Halibut	4,000,000
Miscellaneous	1,400,000
Clams	900,000
Crab	650,000
Shrimp	350,000
Tuna	50,000
	$113,850,000

The salmon pack has declined in recent years and there is much anxiety. Heavy restrictions have had to be placed on the industry, resulting in considerable resentment within and without the Territory. But until annual catches show an upward trend or research results give a different reason for the decline, the hypothesis of overfishing in the past, with consequent need for severe restriction, seems the only sensible view to take. The record output of the salmon fishery was 8,437,603 cases in 1936. In 1948 it had declined to 3,874,540 cases. Presumably by careful, local regulation of the take in the future, the runs can be restored. But this will have to be accomplished in the face of tremendous economic pressure by the fishing industry, which presses always for more liberal regulations and then blames the Fish and Wildlife Service when the fishery declines.

Herring and to some extent halibut likewise have been reduced by overfishing but still contribute a substantial pack. The northward movement of tuna, or albacore, into Alaskan waters promises an increasingly valuable fishery. In addition there exists in the Bering Sea a tremendous population of fishes not now merchantable (mostly flatfishes and cod) which may some day become important.

Far behind the fishery in cash value is the return from furs. Fur trapping occupies 15,000 natives (Eskimos, Indians, and Aleuts) and 5,000 whites seasonally. From an earlier era of gross exploitation, the present industry is one of tacitly accepted conservation methods applied by the Fish and Wildlife Service in the form of legal restrictions on the take. There are no registered trap lines in Alaska, but the existence and inviolability of informally designated lines are generally observed. Trappers alternate their lines or limit their catches to keep the fur species in relative abundance. Research is being conducted at the University of Alaska in conjunction with the Fish and Wildlife Service on the ecology of the fur-bearing species so that an understanding may be reached on the conservation of the habitats and populations of the several species.

It is unlikely, nevertheless, that fur trapping will ever become as important again as it was in the past. The leveling of incomes tends to reduce the market for the expensive furs and makes more significant the "bread and butter" species, such as the muskrat, which has such a high reproductive potential, in addition to the fact that the United States and Alaska have immense areas of suitable muskrat habitat. The fur industry is also to some extent at the mercy of fashion, especially with the more expensive furs. For example, the boom market for silver fox in the 1920's has quite gone. There is also the growing competition of the domesticated rabbit. The 1951 sale of furs from Alaska was only $1,685,846 and until there is a general upward trend in prices it is unlikely that this total can be much increased.

The take of fur seals on the Pribilof Islands is worth much more than the total fur catch of land animals. In 1952, 51,632 three-year-old bulls were killed and their pelts brought $5,067,527. Additional by-products of the seals were sold for $72,869. The story of the recovery of the fur seal herd and of its management is a classic of conservation effort. An interesting recent document on this subject is *The Pribilof Report*, 1949, published by the Department of Interior in 1951.

Other wildlife values

The native ungulate species of the Alaskan fauna—caribou, moose, black-tailed deer, Dall sheep, and mountain goat, are an immensely important resource to which no money values can be given. The problems of their conservation, which are largely problems of conservation of habitat, are discussed at length elsewhere in this report. The meat value to the white population of moose and caribou is at the moment considerable, but will proportionately decline as the human population increases. The sporting value may be expected to rise as the population increases. The esthetic appreciation of the ungulate game is growing and should not be minimized vis-à-vis sporting value. More and more people are coming to Alaska to see these animals in their natural setting and have no desire to shoot them. Consideration for this kind of visitor will be amply repaid in value to the Territory.

The caribou and moose, and to a much lesser extent the Dall sheep, are a very considerable factor in the lives of many Alaskan natives, Eskimo or Indian. Conservation of the stocks is necessary in their interests alone. The animals provide not only necessary food, but many by-products integral in the maintenance of the native cultures.

The Alaskan brown bear is so far famed for its size that it is an object of sport, and of wonder to many whose ambition is merely to observe rather than kill the biggest bear on earth. The animal is omnivorous and no great hindrance to other forms of land use in Alaska, though cattle ranchers on Kodiak—occupants of a very limited area—complain that the Alaskan brown bear is a predator on their stocks. The salmon-fishing interests also complain that the brown bear takes serious toll of the spawning salmon ascending the rivers. One recent report (Shuman, 1950) called for reduction of Kodiak bears on the ground that they were preying rather heavily upon the much reduced runs of red salmon—runs that had been reduced by over-fishing, not by bears. Whereas it is true that considerable salmon are taken by the bears, and even some of the few cattle that exist on Kodiak, the value of the bear as a recreational resource is so great that some deterrent other than killing should be sought in protecting the salmon and cattle. The Fish and Wildlife Service is in fact seeking such a solution.

Besides the brown bear, Alaska is endowed with generous populations of grizzly, black, and polar bears, the latter of which contributes even today to the winter diet of northern Eskimos. Black and grizzly bears are shot rather indiscriminately by Alaskans, despite their nominal status as protected game species, yet both are holding their own in numbers surprisingly well.

Now that commercial whaling in the Alaskan Arctic has ceased, the oceanic mammals are hunted only by the Eskimos. Very few whales are taken now, but such as there are have significance for the Eskimos as food and material. The common seal (*Phoca*) and the bearded seal (*Erignathus*) are also assiduously hunted for food and materials, and as far as we can gather the stocks are in no danger of undue depletion.

The walrus is in a different category. This great mammal, weighing up to 2,750 lbs. or more, feeds on clams which it digs from the sea floor with its canine teeth that have evolved into tusks which may reach 30 inches in length. The Eskimo hunts the walrus for food, dog food, and skins for the large boat—the umiak. The stomach is used as a storage sack and the intestines for various purposes. The ivory is valuable for functional artifacts such as harpoon heads, but more particularly nowadays for ornamental carving. The present price of walrus ivory on the shore is $2 a pound and a moderately good tusk will weigh 7 pounds. For the sake of the ivory alone there is a tendency to hunt more walruses than are needed. The Alaska

Native Service very properly favors the extension of ivory carving as a source of income for the Eskimos, but the conservationist may well hope that the tourist trade in carved ivory will not be developed to the point where the walrus population is endangered. Expansion of the walrus hunt should await the most searching inquiry into populations and life history, made over several years. James Brooks of the University of Alaska is now well started on such an inquiry.

The Territory has an integral position in the waterfowl distribution and migratory system on the North American continent. Here are the breeding grounds for many species seen on the Pacific flyway. Ducks, geese, swans, waders, and sandhill cranes nest in relatively scattered areas about the Territory and on the Arctic slope, but there are also remarkable breeding concentrations, such as the coastal band, several miles deep, along the Bering Sea between the mouths of the Kuskokwim and Yukon rivers. The number of geese on this remote, low, flat tundra is astonishing. In a report on recent surveys of waterfowl breeding in this area, Spencer et al. (1951) note breeding densities of geese and brant averaging 130 birds per square mile, and during the postnesting period they speak of "uncountable" numbers of young gathered along the coast. Besides the 400 square miles of intensively used goose range, there are 20,000 additional square miles of wet tundra in the delta that carry on the average 17 breeding waterfowl to the square mile, mostly ducks. Smaller breeding concentrations occur in various interior flatlands such as along the Yukon River near Fort Yukon and around Minto Lakes near Fairbanks. Various minor river deltas, like that of the Copper River, support smaller numbers.

There is no way of assessing the value of this resource, but it is immense and significant far beyond the boundaries of the Territory. The waterfowl are also important in the economy of the natives and have a sporting value within Alaska.

There is a considerable stock of small game in Alaska, including various kinds of hares, ptarmigans, and grouse. Most of the sport hunting for small game is directed toward snowshoe hares and ptarmigans. However, this is inconsequential compared to the use of small game for food by Eskimos and Indians. Hares and ptarmigans are important food sources during years when they are abundant, but being cyclic they are not as dependable as big game.

The tourist industry

Of increasing importance in the economy of Alaska is the mounting flow of tourists who visit the Territory in summer. With expanding highways and ever improving facilities for travel by air and water, this source of income can well become a major industry, as the Alaska Field Committee has acknowledged (Table 1). A very recent publication by Stanton (1953) thoroughly documents this view. Policies of game and fish management and of park development must heed the needs and tastes of the visiting public.

Many visitors are attracted to Alaska by the reports of fabulous sport fishing. It is axiomatic of course that the more who come to enjoy this sport, the less fabulous the fishing becomes, and it will be no easy task to supply indefinitely into the future, fishing of a quality to attract visitors from afar. Species such as the Dolly Varden trout, which were scorned in the past and even were killed for bounty because of their depredations on salmon eggs and young, can be expected to attain new stature as pressure on other stream fishes increases.

Fewer tourists partake of Alaskan hunting, but their monetary contributions are correspondingly much greater. Countless sportsmen in the United States aspire some day to bag in Alaska a brown bear or one of the great Kenai moose, and as in the case of the sports fishery, the ability of the Fish and Wildlife Service to supply such trophy hunting will condition the numbers of hunters that come in future years.

The majority of tourists, however, are only secondarily interested in hunting and fishing but come to see the scenery, the live animals in the parks, and simply *wild* country. In view of the development of the past decade, it may be more difficult than one would suppose to continue to meet this demand. Preservation of roadsides and camp sites in an attractive condition, free of objectionable advertising, tin can dumps and unsightly shacks, had best be planned now when the task is small rather than a decade or two hence when the cleanup may be staggeringly large. For our part we were distressed by the litter and disorder attending all settlements and even many remote camping places. Whole communities in the northern Lake States and other resort centers have found that maintaining a clean and relatively undisturbed countryside is an essential part of attracting tourists.

There are at present only four National Monuments (Katmai, Glacier Bay, Sitka, and Kasaan) and one National Park (Mount McKinley) set aside to preserve features of tourist interest. There will be need for other such areas, especially in southern Alaska. Some of the National Wildlife Refuges, administered by Fish and Wildlife Service, and various areas under management of the Forest Service and the Bureau of Land Management will serve these needs in part, but the Park Service is specifically equipped to cope with large numbers of recreationalists and they should be fully supported in the effort.

In addition to developing areas for mass recreation, there should be adequate provision for reserving large blocks of country in *wilderness* status, to act as reservoirs of wilderness game and to serve the needs of the more discerning outdoorsmen who wish to get completely away from roads and crowds. At present so much of Alaska is more or less isolated that wilderness preservation may seem to be no problem, but experience in the western United States indicates that wild mountain country can be conquered and tamed with alarming rapidity under the pressure of growing populations. The time to select and set aside wilderness areas is today, before development begins. Parts of Katmai and Glacier Bay National Monuments and of McKinley Park serve the purpose admirably, but these reservations are by no means enough. Wilderness areas should be designated in the national forests of the southeast, in some of the central mountains such as the Kilbuck and Wrangell ranges, and perhaps most importantly in the northern mountain and tundra complex. The eastern Brooks Range sloping down to the Arctic plain on the north and to the Yukon valley on the south would be an ideal Arctic wilderness area. Not only would such a reservation serve to maintain a sample of the primitive northland for posterity, but it could be a base for long-term ecological studies of the Arctic flora and fauna. The scientific importance of reserving such study areas cannot be overemphasized. Subsequent chapters of this report will show that the seemingly remote Arctic has been so changed by fire, reindeer grazing, wolf control, hunting, and fishing that there is shockingly little of it left unaltered.

In short, one of the very characters which makes Alaska attractive to visitors—the remoteness, the wilderness flavor —is by no means assured. The desirability of preserving the wild aspect of the country is in no way contradictory to the acknowledged need for building up the human population and the economic base of the Territory. It is in fact a corollary of encouraging the tourist industry, one of the largest potential sources of income.

Comparative prospects of other resources

AGRICULTURE.—Contention has been warm for 70 years as to whether Alaska could develop a thriving agriculture. Some quite amazing progress has been made in breeding cereals of short growth periods and in working out methods of beating the frost, or increasing the growing period by such devices as spreading coal dust so that the dark-colored surface may absorb heat in spring. But a thriving agriculture has not yet materialized.

About 15,000 acres are now in cultivation in the Territory. The three main areas of farming activity are the Tanana Valley around Fairbanks, the Matanuska Valley north of Anchorage, and the western part of Kenai Peninsula. The climate of the Tanana Valley is definitely continental, with very cold winters, permafrost below 18 inches, and quite delightful short balmy summers with a good deal of sunshine. The Matanuska Valley does not enjoy quite so good a climate as the Tanana region but has a slightly longer growing season. Kenai Peninsula has the longest growing season, of 104 to 112 days, but the climate is largely sunless in summer.

Wherever crops are grown in Alaska, large quantities of fertilizers are needed and must be applied each year. It would seem that the biological processes in the soil producing plant food are not active enough to meet the demands of plants which, after all, have been selected for their high metabolic capacity. The traumatic shock of clearing the ground also upsets the nitrogen cycle. The slack has to be taken up with readily assimilable inorganic salts. This great expense puts a second handicap on farming activity, temperature being the first. The market for Alaskan-grown produce such as truck vegetables, potatoes, poultry and eggs, and fresh milk is larger than can be supplied, and prices are good. The Matanuska Valley Cooperative alone sells $1,500,000 worth of produce per annum.

Nevertheless, full-time farmers are very few indeed. It is our opinion that such agricultural development as is possible in Alaska—which is more limited than the enthusiasts would imply—is being hampered by the national preoccupation with the homesteading style of development. Agriculture in Alaska gets but little help from the weather so that the homesteading does not develop in the way it did in the prairie states or in California. Many of the homesteading efforts we saw in the Kenai Peninsula were pitiful and pathetic, and we had little opinion of the soil as being worth the effort of clearing. Homesteading and lack of capital are nearly synonymous, yet this type of terrain which is so niggard in natural gifts needs a very large initial expenditure of capital to be made into commercially productive land.

The time for work on the land in Alaska is during the summer; but the homesteader is unable to work on the land at that time because he must earn money to keep going and the demand for labor is highest in the summer. The homesteader with little or no capital is sentencing himself and his wife to a life of hard labor, for he will never catch up with himself. We feel that if men with a good deal of capital were to begin farming operations in certain parts of Alaska, they might well get a reasonable but not a large return in the not too distant future. Take, for example, a dairy-farming operation in the Tanana Valley. There is the clearing of the ground and the wait through a few unproductive years until it gets thawed out and changed to arable soil. A considerable area would be much more economical to clear than the small patch a homesteader might be able to afford. Then there are the buildings; as the cows have to be housed for eight months of the year, it would be preferable to build a large covered court, allowing the dehorned cows freedom within it, and putting in bedding at frequent intervals. The body of manure building up under the cows produces considerable heat, and when the cows go to grass again, the manure has been conserved in the court and is available for mechanical spreading on the land. A large herd of cows, machine milked, would be much more economical to establish and maintain than the homesteader's two or three. But such an operation would need a very large initial capital outlay and the fact is that people with large capital are not ready to venture it on Alaskan agriculture.

It seems clear that in so far as the Matanuska Experiment has been successful, it has been because the federal government bore the initial expense of clearing and building a properly designed set of buildings. Even so, the 160-acre unit is probably far too small for an efficient farming operation in Alaska.

Reindeer grazing, which is biologically sound in that it uses an animal adapted to the terrain and does not attempt artificial moulding of the terrain to the animal, is discussed in expanded form later in this report. The experiment failed in Alaska through lack of foresight into the desired scope of the industry, and the lack of observation and interpretation of range conditions. Future reindeer grazing development is to be desired, but because such vast areas have been overgrazed in the past fifty years, a return will be slow and will have little effect on the meat supply in Alaska for many years.

The pastoralism of the commoner domesticated animals in Alaska has not reached considerable proportions, mainly because areas where year-round grazing is possible are few, and not of great extent. The development of a pastoral industry does not take place when there are only small pockets of a few tens of thousands of acres for grazing. Beef cattle are being grazed on Kodiak Island with moderate success. Numbers are between 1,000–2,000, the individual ranchers owning from 100–800 head apiece. It is said there are also 1,000 head of cattle running wild on Chirikof Island.

From time to time sheep have been grazed on some islands of the Aleutian chain, Unimak Island, Umnak, Unalaska, Adak, and Sitkalidak Island (near Kodiak). The only important success has been on Umnak. We suggest that the possibilities for cattle and sheep ranching in the Aleutian chain should be explored more vigorously than in the past, and that close attention should be given to the breeds used. The wet climate of the Aleutian Islands is not suitable for sheep of Merino derivation, and it is probable that animals with a habit of dispersal rather than of close flocking would thrive better on terrain devoid of predators. The Scottish Mountain Blackface breed is one which receives no adventitious food in a hilly country often poorer in quality than the volcanic islands of the Aleutian chain. The Cheviot breed, which has done so well on the Falkland Islands, might be tried also. Difficulties of travel and marketing may, of course, cut out possibility of success on the Aleutian chain, even if pastoralism were biologically feasible.

The presence of grass in any habitat is no criterion that pastoralism will be successful. There are areas of abundant grass in Alaska, such as in the Tanana and Matanuska valleys, but as the Department of Agriculture's (1949) *Report on Exploratory Investigations of Agricultural Problems of Alaska* pointed out, these native grasses cannot withstand close grazing or repeated cutting for hay. Nonnative grasses have been imported and in some places have become naturalized. Success of managed grassland will depend on a cheaper source of fertilizer than is available at present.

FORESTRY.—It has been estimated that there are 116,000 square miles of forest land in Alaska—a fifth of the whole area of the Territory. H. J. Lutz (1950) estimates that one-fifth of this area supports marketable timber and that the rest should be left alone to realize its great value as wildlife habitat and to meet some opportunity in the distant future when utilization of low-grade stands may be possible. We would also wish to express the opinion that large areas of interior scrub forest should be left alone because they are beautiful and have great value for recreation. By recreation is not meant necessarily the opportunity to litter the forest with beer cans and explode firearms irresponsibly, but that mankind living in modern conditions of civilization shall have areas of retreat where there can be re-creation of spirit. The important tourist industry in Alaska will be contingent in part upon maintenance of attractive landscape, which includes timberland as well as wildlife and mountain scenery.

The Tongass and Chugach National Forests contain most of the marketable timber and consist of Sitka spruce, western hemlock and western red cedar. Production of saw timber in 1947 was 80,000,000 board feet. Settlers, miners, and residents cut for personal use 754,000 board feet in 1949. The estimated timber stand on the Tongass Forest is 78,500,000,000 board feet, and on the Chugach, 6,260,-000,000 board feet.

One of the most promising developments in Alaskan forestry is the pulp mill operation at Ketchikan. The concession should allow the mill to produce 500 tons of pulp a day for eighty years. Clear felling of staggered 40 acre lots will be practiced, and the indications from earlier small fellings are that the forests should maintain production indefinitely on the basis of an eighty-year rotation. The forests of southeastern Alaska probably could easily produce something more than 1,000,000 tons of pulp annually.

Forestry is more likely to attract and maintain a high permanent population than most other Alaskan natural resources.

The fact remains that the large part of Alaska's forests will have their highest practical value as wildlife habitat and their conservation should be no less constant because of that.

MINERALS.—The most important mineral mined in Alaska is gold, production being 279,988 ounces in 1947. Practically all the gold is obtained from placer deposits, some of which lie beneath immense overloads of loess. This overload is being washed away into the rivers by powerful hoses and the placer dredge detritus scars the landscape after the gravel has been washed. The world's largest lode mine, at Juneau, is now closed down.

Two-thirds of the silver recovered comes as a by-product of gold mining; one-third comes from lead ore. Very little copper is now produced since the Copper River mines were closed in 1938.

Platinum is mined in the Goodnews Bay area of southwestern Alaska in quantities around 20,000 troy ounces per annum. Tin, zinc, lead and antimony are also mined in Alaska. The production of coal is between 350,000 and 450,000 tons per annum, mostly lignitic, but one-fifth of the coal mined is of high grade. All of the output is used within the Territory. The estimated value of the 1949 output was $3,000,000.

Oil exists in Alaska, but in what quantities is not generally known, as exploration is done by the Navy through Arctic contractors and the results have not been published.

The total cash value of all mineral products produced in 1949 was only $15,302,000 (Stanton, 1953), scarcely one-eighth the value of the fishery.

WATER POWER.—Explorations of water power potentialities indicate a possible 200 dam sites in southern Alaska that collectively could produce over one million horsepower.

Appropriations for the Eklutna project of 30,000 kilowatt capacity have already been made. Development of water power is urgently needed in the Territory and agricultural development may be said to wait upon it, because synthesis of calcium nitrate, drawing on the nitrogen of the air and the vast deposits of limestone in the Territory, by using hydroelectric power, would be the obvious way to reduce the price of agricultural nitrate from its present severely limiting price of 25–27 cents a pound. However, dam construction is a serious potential danger to the salmon runs and should be planned with the welfare of the salmon fishery in mind.

Summary

Despite the favorable comparisons made in brochures and in pictures of large tomatoes and dairy herds at pasture, Alaska is a cold Arctic and sub-Arctic country. The limiting factor of temperature has kept economic development at such a low level that the total population of the Territory was only 72,524 in 1939, of which about half were natives. The total population in 1950 was 128,643, in which the native population had remained almost static, implying an influx of 56,000 people in eleven years—more than 150 per cent of the 1939 white population. There can be few so blindly optimistic as to suggest that this expansion is the result of normal development depending on the res urces of the Territory. Rather it is a direct function of defense spending. Any sudden advance into a condition of world peace would topple this ten-year mushroom development. The true consolidated pace of Alaskan economic development depending on wise use of the Territory's own resources, cannot be rapid, and laying aside the rose-colored spectacles, it is unlikely that any considerable proportion of the land can change from production of wild game, fur, and timber to any more artificial usage.

It has been said that what Alaska needs most is people and that the population should be boosted to the half-million mark as rapidly as possible. We agree that certain kinds of administrative and economic problems are easier to approach when there is a large body of people to administer for, but any expectation of a rapid increase to the half-million mark based on the natural resources and industry of the country would be quite unrealistic. Industrial development, as typified by the salmon and sea food canneries, the Ketchikan pulp mills and the proposed Skagway aluminum smelting plant, are peripheral. This leaves Arctic Alaska and the vast interior largely as it is at present. Mining in the interior is not a very large operation, and the mechanical techniques developed are such as to employ relatively few men, at high income rates, for seven months of the year. The Nome mining area, important as it is and will be, is again peripheral. We can expect the interior to be virtually left alone for a long time yet, though certain influences of man will continue to have their effects on different game animals, as described later, and these influences may well be critical for the animals. The interior has been and is constantly being penetrated by such men as prospectors and trappers, but no radical change in land use generally can be expected.

As the situation is at present contrived, the wildlife resources of the Territory are the most important ones and over half the population depends on them almost entirely for existence. There are comparatively few people in Alaska unaffected by the status of wildlife. The situation may be expected to change, lessening the direct importance of wildlife to the country's economy, but even then, indifference to the fate of the wildlife would be rank improvidence. We believe that Alaska's scenery, remoteness, and wildlife can be her greatest continuing resource, in that tourism could well become one of the prime industries which will directly supplement her principal income now derived from the salmon fishery. The attraction of Alaska for the tourist will not be the man-made amusements of a Miami but the beauties of natural habitats and their denizens, maintained through conservation. The degraded habitat of the ecological climax broken through human misuse carries none of the joy and rehabilitative quality of the truly natural scene.

If our analysis of the problem is correct, the government agencies which bear the burden of conserving fisheries, wildlife, scenery, and forests, are in fact carrying the major responsibility for Alaska's future economy. The problems of big game management which we discuss in the pages that follow must in this light be construed as major problems, vital to the Territory, and therefore deserving of the most careful study and management.

4

NATIVE PEOPLES IN RELATION
TO WILDLIFE

THE IMPACT of a technological culture, with a firm belief in its own progress, on a hunting-food-gathering people is usually to the detriment of the simpler culture. The influence of western civilization on the native peoples of Alaska has been no exception to the rule. Eskimos of the western and northern coasts, Aleuts of the Aleutian chain, and Indians of the interior and southern Alaska, have all suffered degradation in one way or another, and interference with the wildlife resources on which they depended was one of the initial, as well as one of the continuing factors in the breakup of their way of life. The repair of former damage is the general and sincere desire, though the methods of achieving such an end do not seem to be based on a clear understanding of the problems and therefore show little coordination.

Our mission in Alaska has been concerned primarily with the status of wildlife in the Territory and we have chosen to build our short investigation mainly on the basis of caribou, moose, and reindeer in relation to range, and what man and the animals are doing to this immense expanse of range. Nevertheless, we have been compelled to consider the lot of Alaskan native peoples in relation to our main problem as if they were part of the indigenous fauna, and this without the slightest disrespect to them. Indeed, this is the only possible scientific approach for us. The limitations of time and of our terms of reference preclude any profound anthropological treatment of the Alaskan native problem, but the integration of the native situation, as we have seen it, with the problems of wildlife conservation, demands some socioecological discussion.

Impacts of alien cultures

The problem began with the Russian movement westward along the Aleutian chain in the eighteenth century. There were massacres, cruelties, and injustices, followed by some deplorable conduct on the part of British and American seafaring men, but it is worthy of note that Baranof, the first Russian resident governor of Alaska, earned respect and even affection from the Aleuts, and ruled the coasts as far as Sitka with a standard of justice ahead of his time. Russia came to Alaska for furs, and from our reading of the history it would seem that one of the major upsets to Aleut culture as a result of Russian exploitation, and following the earlier massacres, was the movement of people. Baranof's expeditions to Kodiak and Sitka and the intervening coasts involved large fleets of *bidarkas* and many hundreds of Aleut men. There were often losses at sea, there were losses in fights with the fiercer Indians of the southeast, and losses from disease on a scale unknown before. Enforced movement and migration led finally to concentration around white communities, with consequent dependence on them.

The Russians also began what was in effect a process of absorption by miscegenation and we understand that recent blood-group testing of the Aleut population shows an average of 15 per cent of non-Aleut blood. This admixture may have helped to make the Aleut more amenable to the adoption of a way of life nearer the white man's in character, but possibly more important has been the native social structure of Aleut communities which has developed as a result of marked insulation. The island communities developed a definite village life, and leadership emerged to a degree it never has done in the sister people, the Eskimos. These several factors have brought the Aleut to a readier state for smooth absorption than has been the case with the Eskimo and the Indian. From west to east along the Aleutian chain and the Alaska Peninsula, the process of cultural absorption and adaptation is much more apparent.

The salmon canneries are the source of prosperity to the Aleut, so it is natural that the people on or nearer to the base of the Alaska Peninsula should have adopted the American way of life most completely. The lot of Aleuts farther down the Aleutian chain is varied; the pastoralism of sheep on a few of the islands might be thought to provide for the people something of what the canneries do farther east, but this does not seem to be the case. In fact it is the opinion of competent observers that the sheep have a depressing and depopulating effect, in that the sheep ranches are worked by the natives, but profits do not accrue to them, nor do adequate wages. Similarly, reindeer pastoralism on some of the islands has failed to provide a sustaining industry, but that matter will be discussed in a later chapter.

The boats owned by some of these communities, given to them at some earlier date, are unsuited to the conditions and are not used unless the sea is settled and calm. The sea, therefore, is not contributing to the economy of the insular Aleuts as it should, except on the Pribilofs where the fur seal industry is supporting the natives in a most commendable manner. For the most part, however, the Aleuts are caught between the two worlds of land and sea, reaping from neither as is their natural right. We feel that the socioeconomic situation and the pastoral industry, such as it is, on the Aleutian chain should be the subject of special investigation and that the undoubted natural and pastoral resources should be integrated to the welfare of the Aleut people. They have shown themselves able to follow a pastoral industry and seaward fishing and hunting if they are given opportunity without being economically handicapped. As the situation now stands, the handicaps are too great for the Aleuts to achieve an independent prosperity for themselves.

The history of the Kenai, Prince William Sound, and southeastern Alaskan Indians shows that they were less amenable to servitude and absorption, and the Russians suffered many tragedies in their initial contacts with these fierce peoples. These Indians fed largely from the produce of the land and the rivers and did not find their food staples influenced by the Russian search for furs. But the northern expansion of American and British interests caught the Indians as by a pincer movement, and perhaps because they were least adjusted to change and adaptation, they suffered worst of the three races. Their culture is now dead and the living descendants of the proud Tlingits live a pathetically tamed life in rather squalid frame-hut villages around the canneries or in poorer "downtown" parts of the white men's towns. In some parts of southeastern Alaska the Indians still hunt deer and some are independent fishermen, but like the Aleuts, they are mostly dependent upon wages for a living.

The more primitive Athapaskans of the interior have become trappers absolutely dependent on the rather fickle fur market. Their main food resource of caribou has greatly diminished as a result of frequent burning of winter range since the white man's entry. Before that time, it is known that the Athapaskans practiced scattered rotational burning for the encouragement of moose range, but this local management apparently did not interfere with caribou habitat or abundance. The moose is of increasing importance in the economy of the interior Indians and is likely to continue so, not only for meat but for leather as well. The great rivers pass through their country, making, breaking, and remaking land and developing that green habitat of secondary vegetational succession which is the perfect terrain for moose.

There is a strong tendency for these people to be careless in their husbandry of big game resources, shooting either moose or caribou at any time of year without regard to conservation principles. The scarcity of moose in the vicinity of nearly all Indian settlements in the Yukon drainage is direct evidence of overhunting and of the need for a well directed program of conservation education. Curiously, these people utilize fur resources with much more care and forethought, but this may stem from the feeling of ownership of trap lines and of assured return to the individual from preserving basic breeding stocks of fur animals. No such feeling has yet emerged regarding grazing animals.

The Eskimos of Alaska were affected later than the Aleuts or the southern Indians, in the second half of the nineteenth century. Whaling ships came through the Aleutian chain and Bering Strait, hunting whales for baleen and oil, and walruses for oil and ivory, in the Bering Sea and Arctic Ocean. It is the white man's conception that the seas are free and he felt no compunction whatever in cutting straight into these direct staples of Eskimo culture. Whales were hunted almost to extinction in a thirty-year fishery, and the walrus herds were sorely depleted. Eskimos received firearms from the whalers and though these may have been an immediate advantage under the conditions of declining game populations, their use must have hastened the decline to catastrophe. Caribou, for example, were all but exterminated along the Bering coast and were reduced to scarcity on the Arctic slope to supply the whaling ships which concomitantly were making away with the oceanic mammals.

The whalers also brought tuberculosis, venereal disease, and measles, and by the turn of the century the Eskimos had been reduced to conditions of sore distress. The cessation of whaling and the introduction of reindeer must have given respite, so that this remarkably skilled and truly cooperative people saved both their race and their culture. Their own technological achievements, adapting them perfectly to life in the unbroken complex of the difficult Arctic and sub-Arctic environment, were so remarkable that the white man was willing to learn from the Eskimo. He is still doing so. Furthermore, the Eskimo has never felt himself inferior to the white man and has therefore preserved a status which at this time may well carry him forward into the future economy of Alaska as the accepted equal partner of the white man.

That stage is far from having been reached and it is our impression that the United States as an administrative power has not fully made up its mind how to handle the Eskimo problem. Thus we see at one time an Eskimo village such as Mekoryuk on Nunivak Island, run well by the people themselves and cared for wisely and kindly by the Alaska Native Service; then the most northerly village of Barrow, where there is the unique concentration of Eskimos to the number of about a thousand persons, full of prosperity and punch as a result of the Navy Petroleum Reserve Base at Point Barrow, but housing themselves in almost unbelievably unsanitary conditions. The village of Bethel on the Kuskokwim River does not seem to have any real purpose for existence there now; it was a more prosperous settlement in the days when the river was a more important waterway. Bethel is squalid in the extreme, and the condition of the Eskimos in such a place is pathetic. The incidence of tuberculosis is appalling and can scarcely be otherwise with housing at the standard it is on a site but a few inches above, and sometimes below, the water table.

The Eskimos of the Kuskokwim and Yukon rivers are now utterly dependent on the white man's economy, but they have not been raised to equal partakers of his standard of living. The men go away to the canneries every summer or to the Railroad to sell their labor, but there seems little help and guidance for these people in the matter of spending money wisely. There is hardship in these villages every winter, despite the fact that the men earned good wages while away in the summer.

Utilization of wildlife resources

In recent years the Eskimos have tended more and more to work for white man's wages, at least part of the year, and to concentrate in stable village communities where the opportunity for working is better. But they still retain a strong tendency to hunt and fish for part of their living. Seals, walrus, caribou, fur animals, birds, and various fishes contribute importantly to Eskimo economy. Likewise the semidomestic reindeer is a critical factor in the feeding and clothing of some communities, despite its present greatly curtailed status. In addition to preserving traditions of hunting, the Eskimos have succeeded to a remarkable degree in preserving their handicrafts, many of which are associated with the hunt. Manufacture of skin boats, skin clothing, and bone and ivory implements has not been altered materially, although in housing and some items of clothing the Eskimos have tended to follow the habits of the white man.

In respect to utilization of wild animals Eskimos are no more provident than the Indians, and given the opportunity they frequently kill more than they really need. It does not appear to us that the Eskimo has any understanding of or regard for the idea of conservation. We have enough evidence to satisfy us that modern Eskimo hunting of caribou, walrus, and wildfowl is often very wasteful, but we do not wish in any way to condemn the Eskimo for this. His extremely unabstract, practical philosophy, and ability to live in the present have not fitted him in his own culture to indulge in reflection on the dynamics of animal populations or to consider questions of conservation from a developed point of view. If a group of caribou is trapped on a point in the Arctic Ocean, the Eskimo will go on shooting, often very wildly, until all the animals are dead or the ammunition is exhausted. The bow and arrow stage of culture was conserving because of its limitations; the rifle has removed these limitations, but there has been no development of philosophy to offset the technological advance. It will become necessary to convey the ideas of conservation to the Eskimos, but it will not be done by proscription or curtailment of their freedoms as hunters and food gatherers. Solution of this problem will come from patient contacts of men and women with anthropological and psychological training who are aware of the principles of conservation. Such work will be often unrewarding and must inevitably be slow. But it should be undertaken as a major objective of the education program now so well begun by the Alaska Native Service.

The animal life of Eskimo Alaska is much less persecuted at the moment than it was fifty years ago. On the Arctic slope there are many more land animals, such as caribou and moose, and fewer hunters than were found by Stefansson (1913) and other visitors to the Arctic coast at the beginning of this century. This is due in part to reduction in numbers of Eskimos by disease and in part to the shift from complete to only partial dependence on wildlife. Especially has there been a decrease in inland hunting by the coastal peoples, now largely settled in permanent villages. Along the Arctic Ocean there is now no occupied native village between Barrow and Barter Island.

There is only one inland group of Eskimos left, the Nunamiut of the Anaktuvuk Pass region of the Alaskan Arctic, comprising 12 families and 71 people in all (Rausch, 1951). The Nunamiut are nomadic and still depend largely on the caribou for their sustenance. Their demands are heavy, caribou being needed for food for themselves and their dogs; for hides, tents, sleeping bags and harness; for skins from which to make clothing. The actual killing of the caribou by the Nunamiut may be done with no more regard for conservation than elsewhere, but they are so few in number as to impose a nominal drain on the game of this region.

Mature bulls are mainly sought because of their degree of fat storage, and their hides are best for tentmaking. Rausch says each house needs 20 hides, which may last three years. Cows' and calves' skins are needed for clothing. Even the warble-fly larvae are eaten when the caribou happen to be killed in May. On the occasions when the caribou move away from these people's orbit entirely, the Nunamiut hunt Dall sheep or move into the sparse spruce forest south of the Brooks Range seeking moose. They also hunt wolves as part of their livelihood, for the bounty and to trade surplus skins with coastal Eskimos who cannot catch enough for their own needs.

The subject of wildlife in the economy of Alaska natives has been well reviewed by Scott (1951). He brings out convincingly that Eskimo cash income cannot be taken as a criterion for degree of dependence on wildlife resources. His figures also show the tendency of the modern Eskimo population to concentrate, and how the Eskimos and Indians still greatly outnumber the whites in Arctic Alaska, in a ratio of approximately 12:1.

In developing a wildlife conservation program for Alaska, the needs of the various native peoples should be generously considered. It is important that the conservation concept be incorporated into the thinking of the natives, but the idea should be perpetuation of the game for the use of natives and whites together and not just reservation of hunting rights for whites, a notion that is entertained by some Alaskan sportsmen. As intimated above, native hunting today does not seem to us to be excessive except in a few specific situations, such as in the case of moose along the Yukon, and there is no reason to treat this problem as of major importance in accounting for present trends in numbers of grazing animals. Indeed, anxiety should be concentrated on conservation of the winter ranges of the several species—a much more pressing problem. We see no justification at present for any additional checks on the toll of caribou taken by the Eskimos north of the Arctic Circle, for we think such toll may be to the good of the caribou. It is certainly good for the Eskimo, for it helps to maintain him as a free and healthy organism, and to keep active his arts, crafts, and skills. Rausch states that no tuberculosis is apparent as yet in the Nunamiut, whereas the over-all rate in coastal Eskimos and those of the Yukon-Kuskokwim area is around $33\frac{1}{3}$ per cent.

Summary

We consider that the impact of native peoples on the wildlife of the Territory does not preclude its effective conservation at the present time and may, in fact, be locally beneficial. Conversely, we think that the influence of the wildlife crop on the native is wholly to his benefit, helping to provide him with a correct diet rich in protein and fat, and integrating his life and activities. The relationship of the native and his quarry is on the whole almost symbiotic, and in so far as he has relinquished dependence on the wildlife, his health and social life have deteriorated. If the native peoples increase in numbers and diffuse beyond the present distribution, and slowly accept the white man's way of life, they will have to accept the same limitations in relation to game as the white man does, but that stage has not been reached.

5

THE STATUS OF THE CARIBOU

THE caribou (*Rangifer arcticus*) was originally the most widespread and much the most numerous of Alaskan big game mammals. It occupied virtually all of the Territory north of the zone of heavy timber, though of course not in uniform density. Dramatic migrations of herds estimated in astronomical numbers have been described in Alaskan literature since white man first began the exploration of the northlands. Perhaps the very drama of encountering a moving herd led to somewhat exaggerated ideas of actual caribou numbers. Two characteristics of caribou which particularly attract attention are the gregarious habit, which results in formation of very large herds, and the never-ending restlessness of the herds, which may move for hundreds and even thousands of miles in a year. One group of animals, seen and reported by a number of observers in different watersheds, might well create an illusion of abundance. This happens even today but must have been the more true in earlier times when travel and communication were slow and uncertain.

Be that as it may, there certainly were more caribou in central and southern Alaska originally than there are today, although we shall perhaps never know how many more. Today we are struggling to guard and restore mere scattered remnants of the southern herds. In the north, however, caribou are still relatively abundant and secure, and there remains an excellent opportunity for perpetuation and management of the species.

Changes in caribou numbers

The accompanying map (Figure 2) shows the original and the present caribou ranges in Alaska. The greatest loss in occupied range, and in numbers as well, has been in the south and on the lowlands adjoining the Bering Sea in the west. Caribou are gone from the Kenai Peninsula, the lower Susitna basin, the Kilbuck Mountains, the whole tremendous sweep of the Kuskokwim-Yukon delta region, and from Seward Peninsula. Likewise Unimak, Nunivak and Nelson islands have all lost their caribou. Scarce indeed are the herds that remain south of the Arctic Circle, in such scattered localities as the Alaska Peninsula, the Alaska Range and basins of the upper Susitna, Copper, and Tanana rivers.

Furthermore, these surviving remnants in the south no longer wander in nomadic fashion but seem confined to specific, relatively small units of range as designated on the map. That is not to say that they have ceased to migrate. The Alaska Peninsula caribou, by way of example, winter on the rolling tundra around Becharof Lake and summer along the Bering coast near Port Moller 200 miles to the west. The herd of about 2,500 animals makes this round trip regularly, very much as some deer and elk populations

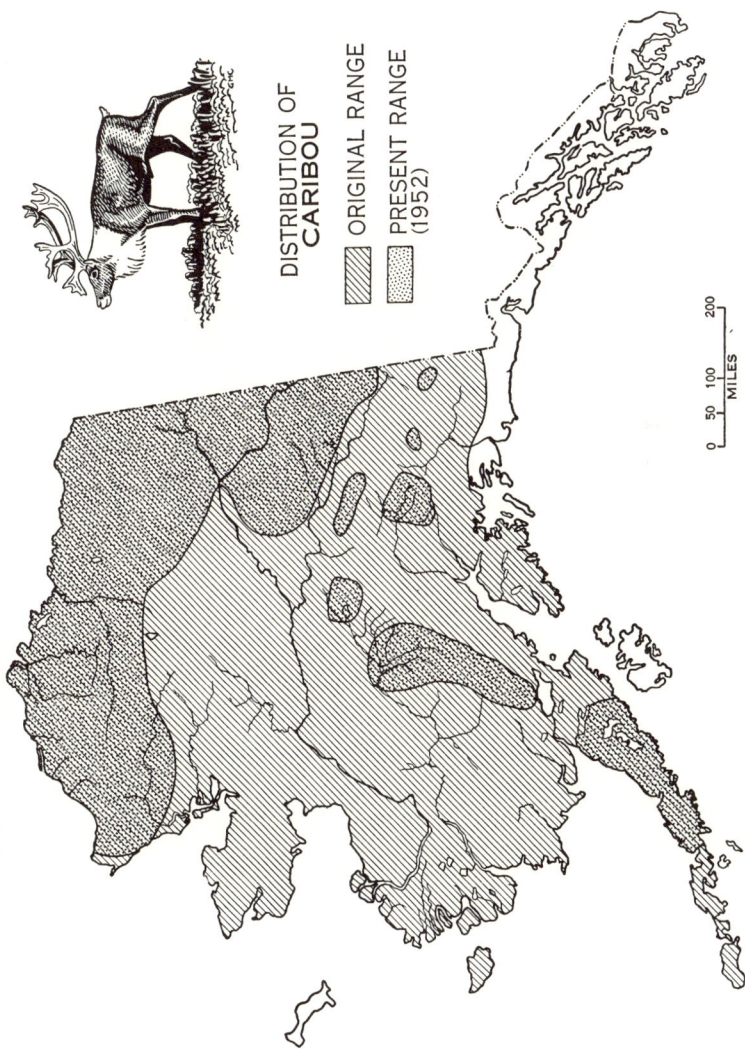

DISTRIBUTION OF CARIBOU

ORIGINAL RANGE

PRESENT RANGE (1952)

0 50 100 200
MILES

FIGURE 2. Original and present ranges of the caribou in Alaska, showing shrinkage of area occupied in central and southern regions.

move systematically between specific summer and winter ranges. Similarly, the Nelchina herd, now numbering about 7,000, winters in the sparse spruce timber northwest of Lake Louise in the upper Susitna drainage and summers regularly in the high glacial valleys of the Talkeetna Mountains. These are local, specific migrations in contrast to the much longer, unpredictable movements of the large northern herds. It seems essential to our discussion, therefore, that the southern and northern caribou be considered separately, so great are the differences in ranges, numbers and behavior of the animals, and of the management problems. The line which seems best to separate these geographic and ecologic regions is the Arctic Circle.

Decrease of caribou south of the Arctic Circle

Some of the largest caribou herds of the past lived in the southern range. As late as 1921, O. J. Murie (1935) computed the Yukon-Tanana herd to be 568,000 animals. Although the data which formed the basis for this figure were meager, it was clear that the herd was very large. There were other southern herds as well for which no specific, numerical estimates were made, but Murie surmises that in Alaska and Yukon Territory together there were somewhere between one and two million caribou, and his map indicates that at least three-quarters of these were south of the Arctic Circle. Dr. Murie was kind enough to recheck for us his original data, and he finds no reason to question his original conclusions.

In the same region the numbers of caribou existing today are fairly accurately known as a result of repeated aerial surveys conducted in late winter by personnel of the Fish and Wildlife Service. Figures reported in 1950 by Scott,

Chatelain, and Elkins, and repeated here in Table 3, show that the collective population of southern caribou comprises ten herds totalling 21,450 animals. However rough the early estimates may have been, it is clear that there has been a material decrease in the population, the causes of which we should attempt to understand in guiding efforts at restoration and management.

Factors that may have had a bearing on this loss of caribou are (1) direct kill by hunting, (2) changes in the range, and (3) changes in predator pressure. Every student of the problem weighs and evaluates these factors differently. Our interpretation is as follows.

Past hunting loss

There is abundant proof that indiscriminate hunting was the first, and for a time the most important, depressant of caribou populations following exploration and settlement of Alaska. Not only did the white trappers, traders, ships' crews, and prospectors depend heavily upon caribou to feed themselves and their dogs, but they supplied the Indians and Eskimos with guns and ammunition which led to even greater slaughter. It is quite unnecessary for us to document this tragic chapter in history—it resembled in general outline the treatment of the bison on the prairies or the elk in the Rocky Mountains. But there were differences.

The difficulty of transport in interior Alaska interfered seriously with the systematic exploitation of resources, including game. Whereas caribou were all but wiped out of the coastal regions and were much reduced on the Arctic plain, there remained until the eventual arrival of conservation consciousness a substantial reservoir of caribou in the

TABLE 3. Numbers of caribou in Alaska in 1948–49, based on aerial counts by technicians of the Fish and Wildlife Service (Scott, Chatelain and Elkins, 1950)

Herds south of the Arctic Circle	*Numbers of caribou*	
Alaska Peninsula	2,500	
Mulchatna	1,000	
Rainy Pass	2,000	
McKinley—Minchumina	5,000	
Wood—Delta River	300	
Mount Sanford	50	
White River	100	
Nelchina	4,000 [1]	
Steese	5,000	
Forty-mile	1,500	
		21,450
Herds north of the Arctic Circle		
Chandalar	20,000	
Anaktuvuk—Upper Koyukuk	9,000	
Upper Colville	7,000	
Kobuk—Noatak	100,000 [2]	
Point Hope—Point Lay	3,000	
		139,000
Total for Alaska...............................		160,450

[1] Increased to 7,000 in 1951 (see Table 4).
[2] This herd was estimated from the ground and the figure may have been too high. No herd of similar size has been observed from the air in the past two years.

rugged interior of the Territory. The great Tanana-Yukon herd studied by Murie was one such remnant. The population of the Brooks Range in northern Alaska was another. It would be an exaggeration, therefore, to say that caribou were seriously depleted solely by hunting. At the time when law and order in game regulation were becoming firmly established there was still an adequate stock of caribou in the central part of the Territory which, following the ancestral pattern of random, long movement, might well have restocked the ranges south of the Yukon and along the Bering coast if other factors had remained favorable. Pursuing this point up to the present time, many of the remnant herds in the south are hunted little or not at all, and are being given some protection from predators as well, and still they are not increasing (examples—herds on the Alaska Peninsula, Mulchatna, Rainy Pass, McKinley-Minchumina, and in the Wrangell Mountains). Therefore it is clear that other important factors probably contributed to the original decrease and are preventing current recovery. The two most obvious are burning and reindeer grazing of the caribou winter ranges.

Changes in range conditions

Consider first the nature of winter range required by caribou and the ecologic implications of its disturbance. When snows blanket the ground and herbaceous foliage is virtually all frozen or unavailable, the caribou subsist on a diet dominated by certain of the branching lichens, called "reindeer lichens," and by willow browse, along with such green tips of sedges and forbs as they can dig out of the snow. The most important of the lichens, of the genera *Cladonia* and *Cetraria*, apparently are the basic elements in the winter diet, supplying the necessary nutrients for subsistence and for successful reproduction in the females. These lichens are slow growing members of various climax associations in the boreal flora. They do not occur in muskegs nor in wet tundra but tend to reach maximum abundance as an understory to the sparse white spruce forest on well drained uplands or in the dry tundra on ridges, benches, and knolls. Because of their slow rate of growth (estimated by Palmer, 1945, in Alaska, and by various Scan-

dinavian ecologists at about one-sixteenth of an inch per
annum) the reindeer lichens will withstand only very light
grazing. Fire eliminates them entirely, up to fifty or even
one hundred years being required for their regeneration.
Where fires have burned down to mineral soil, recovery
may take much longer. The status of caribou, therefore,
seems to be intimately associated with the presence of undisturbed climax vegetation of which the lichens are a
prominent part. The caribou itself, then, can be thought of
as a member of a climax biota. It is true that in spring,
summer, and autumn, caribou wander at will over a tremendous variety of vegetational types, from heavy forest to
wet tundra and they do not then require lichens; but these
are not the critical seasons in the life of the animal. The
inherent nomadic wandering of the herds distributes grazing widely over great areas of range, and thus has the effect
of preventing destruction of the lichen climax by the caribou themselves.

Even the most casual inspection of caribou ranges in
Alaska will reveal that there is relatively little climax lichen
growth left south of the Arctic Circle. On the extensive
coastal area of western Alaska which was occupied by great
herds of reindeer in the first third of the present century,
lichens have been all but grazed out. The condensed history of the reindeer industry will be related in subsequent
pages, but the impact of this pastoral adventure on native
caribou needs explanation here. A comparison of Figures
2 and 3 will show with considerable clarity that there are
no longer caribou on the bulk of the former reindeer range.
Reindeer are much like caribou in their choice of winter
foods, and the tremendous herds, grazing year after year
on the same ranges without opportunity to wander away

into new pastures as caribou would have done, effectively reduced the lichen growth to a point where the reindeer themselves "crashed" spectacularly in the 1930's and '40's. Needless to say the caribou have not returned.

In tracing the present western boundary of caribou range, one is impressed in places with the coincidence of the last outposts of caribou and the easternmost boundary of former reindeer range. To take one example, in about 1920 reindeer were established at the base of the Alaska Peninsula and herds estimated at 10,000 or more (Burdick, 1940, counted the herd at 6,500 after the big die-off of 1938–39) occupied the general area of Dillingham-Egegik-Iliamna Lake for over twenty years, or until the mid-1940's. The intensive grazing of the reindeer discouraged caribou from continuing their ancestral migrations from the mainland to the peninsula, and a small herd then existing on the peninsula was "trapped" there, where they still exist. Mainland caribou travel as far down as the north shore of Lake Iliamna and the Peninsula herd comes up about to Naknek Lake, but the breach in range has never closed, as the map shows. In the ensuing years the lichens have recovered perceptibly on the former reindeer range, and quite probably the caribou some day will reoccupy the gap. It is safe to anticipate, we believe, a gradual recovery of many former reindeer ranges as well as this one. But in explaining the present restricted range of caribou in the west of Alaska, the role played by reindeer must be counted of paramount importance.

In central Alaska there were very few reindeer. Caribou by no means have been eliminated, as on reindeer ranges, but their numbers are materially reduced. Here it appears to us that range destruction by fire is principally responsible.

Probably some of the very best original caribou winter range was on the sparsely timbered white spruce uplands of the Yukon and Tanana valleys and in the upper basins of th'e Copper, Susitna and Kuskokwim rivers. On some unburned remnants of this climax type, as for example in the rolling country northwest of Lake Louise (Susitna drainage), we observed some of the heaviest lichen growth to be seen in Alaska today. In original condition, such climax vegetation was extensive in interior Alaska and served to support many caribou.

Although there certainly were lightning and Indian fires before the coming of the white man, there is a large volume of evidence suggesting that fires increased enormously in both size and frequency after settlement. Particularly during the recurrent periods of gold rush, when hordes of feverish miners swarmed over the north, the timber was slashed and burned unmercifully, just as it was at an earlier day in the gold fields of California and Colorado. Even after the mining excitement subsided, a large population of trappers and prospectors stayed on in Alaska, and as a group they were no less careless with fires than the original miners. The question of fire in the Alaskan spruce lands has been intensively studied by H. J. Lutz, from whose report to the First Alaska Science Conference (1950) we quote as follows: "During the past half-century devastating fires have each year swept over very extensive areas of forested land in the Alaskan interior. Accurate information is lacking but it seems well within the realm of probability to suggest that the average acreage burned annually has been at least one million acres and that not more than 20 per cent of the original white spruce forest remains." Billy Short, Forester, connected with the Fairbanks office

of the Bureau of Land Management, agrees with this conclusion and even extends it with the following statement:
"I might add here that prior to 1937 it was not uncommon
for up to 5 million acres of area to burn annually." R. R.
Robinson of the Division of Forestry in a letter (September 3, 1952) supports Lutz's estimate that four-fifths of the
white spruce has burned at least once, and parts of this
area have burned repeatedly.

Our airplane flights over interior Alaska verified the fact
that these statements do not exaggerate the situation. There
is very little of the climax spruce forest left. And with the
fires, the lichens were lost as well as the mature spruce.
The importance of the problem was well described in two
papers by L. J. Palmer entitled "Caribou versus fire in interior Alaska" which were written in 1940 but unfortunately were not published; these manuscripts came into our
hands at the end of our tour (copies supplied by John L.
Buckley, Alaska Cooperative Wildlife Research Unit, College). Palmer had concluded a decade ago that fire was
the principal factor eliminating caribou from central Alaska.
Banfield (1951) reached more or less the same conclusion
in north-central Canada.

In company with Edward F. Chatelain of the Fish and
Wildlife Service, we examined a series of new and old burns
in the upper Susitna basin and compared the lichen growth
(or more properly, lichen absence) on the burns with that
on a block of unburned country which today is the winter
range of the only caribou herd left in that vicinity, the
Nelchina herd. There was no mystery about why caribou
ceased to frequent the burns. There simply was not enough
lichen for them to find a meal through the snow in winter.
Similar observations were made on the Kenai Peninsula

and lower Susitna Valley, where caribou are now gone, and along the slopes of the White Mountains where the reduced Yukon-Tanana herd ranges. Palmer (*op. cit.*) had stated earlier: "Caribou were reported as plentiful on the Kenai Peninsula in 1890. The first big fire occurred on the Peninsula in 1871, a second one in 1891, and the third in 1910. The last caribou was seen in 1906. In Susitna Valley widespread and recurrent fires occurred at about the same time as on the Kenai Peninsula. Here the last caribou was reported . . . near Fish Lake by a Land Office survey party in 1914."

We do not claim to have looked at any large part of the original winter range of interior caribou, but on the samples which we did inspect, fire had played so dominant a part in destroying the lichen range that we feel quite safe in attaching to that one factor the major blame for caribou decrease. In short, we arrived independently at the conclusion reached earlier by Palmer, again by Banfield, and doubtless by others.

This situation prompts us to suggest that a survey be made of the remaining habitable winter ranges for caribou in southern and central Alaska, and that once these areas are mapped, a fire protection program be worked out jointly between the Fish and Wildlife Service and the Division of Forestry, Bureau of Land Management. The Fish and Wildlife Service might well divert some of its funds to support fire control on key areas of range. From the standpoint of caribou management it is probably much more important that critical lichen ranges be protected from burning than that the already effective program of protecting the herds from hunting and predation be expanded. We cannot agree with the viewpoint expressed by Green (1950) that because Alaska is large and funds for the management of game are small it necessarily follows that the game program "must be directed toward controlling the action of predators, both men and wolves, rather than in improving the game range." To ignore range limitations for caribou is to ignore the crux of the problem. One fire easily could undo the work of decades in protecting a local caribou population from men and wolves.

Wolf predation

The control of wolves, and in recent years of coyotes, has constituted a prominent part of the restoration program for big game in Alaska. Since 1915 the Territorial government has paid substantial bounties on wolf and coyote scalps, amounting in the aggregate to over half a million dollars (Green, 1950). In 1943, federal game agents of the Fish and Wildlife Service began supplementary control measures and at present nine men are so employed. This force concentrates its activities in areas where predation is judged to be critical. By the use of traps, poison, cyanide guns, and by shooting from airplanes, an intensity of local control has been achieved that was impossible under the bounty system alone. Much of this control is directed toward protection of caribou. In view of the present limitations in caribou range, discussed in the foregoing section, we feel obliged to point out certain potential dangers in overextending this activity.

The wolf is indeed the only important predator of caribou and it habitually preys upon the herds, especially in winter. Coyotes, which are increasing in southern Alaska, and perhaps other large carnivores like bears and wolverines, may catch an occasional calf, but such losses are minor compared to the depredations of wolves. The fact that wolves follow the caribou in their peregrinations and leave along the way the carcasses of many calves, and some adults as well, is so well-known that we need not document it here. But appraising the importance of this loss and its effect upon the welfare of the caribou is by no means simple. In situations where hunting is removing the full annual surplus of caribou, or more than the surplus as happened in years past, additional losses to wolves can rightly be considered deleterious. Conversely, under light hunting or no hunting, wolf predation may in the long run be a distinct benefit to caribou by preventing overpopulation and range damage. Thus in each locality the effects of wolf predation on caribou must be judged in the light of the existing balance between the caribou and their range.

Looking at the caribou ranges south of the Arctic Circle, we have seen that the western portions have been all but destroyed by reindeer and the central portions four-fifths destroyed by fire. The capacity of this region to support caribou, therefore, is tremendously circumscribed in comparison to the past, and it is manifest that the original great herds can never be restored by regulating such decimating factors as hunting and predation. Deciding where wolves (and hunting for that matter) need more stringent control finally must resolve upon an examination of local winter ranges in relation to current caribou numbers to see if, in terms of the range, an increase in herd size is desirable. If so, then the numbers of wolves and their role in suppressing numbers of caribou should come under scrutiny, leading perhaps to control. But on ranges fully stocked with caribou, intensive wolf control may not be at all the right thing to do unless adequate hunting pressure is substituted for predation as a population control. Let us consider a specific example.

The Nelchina caribou herd is one of the most important remaining herds in southern Alaska because of its accessibility to hunters from Anchorage. The population of about 4,000 animals in 1948 had been built up to 7,000 in 1951 by intensive wolf control, as indicated in Table 4.

TABLE 4. Increased calf survival and increase in total caribou numbers in the Nelchina herd following inception of intensive wolf control by the Fish and Wildlife Service

Year	Numbers of caribou in herd (aerial counts)	Estimated hunting removal	Per cent calves	Wolf removal	
				By F.W.S.	Other [1]
1948	4,000(?)	?	?	23	
1949	4,500–5,000	400	10	54	50–60
1950	5,000–5,500	500	12.8	58	
1951	7,000	500 +	15.7	33	
				168	50–60

[1] Bounty payments by the Territorial government.

The hunting take is only about 500 animals a year, or 7 to 8 per cent, and the calf count is up as a result of wolf removal, all of which points to continued increase in the herd. Now the real question is, how far should this herd be increased? In examining the winter range, in company with Edward Chatelain (who gathered most of the statistics presented in Table 4), it was obvious to us all that the lichens were being fairly heavily used. The winter range is limited in extent, being a block of unburned taiga surrounded by many burns of varying sizes and ages. As far as we know, any further increase in the Nelchina herd will have to be accommodated on the present winter range; there is nowhere else for the animals to go. Can the existing range support more animals? If so, how many more? Not one of us could answer these questions, and until we *know* how to evaluate caribou range, to what extent are we justified in risking a build-up of numbers on the chance that the animals will somehow distribute themselves so as not to damage the remaining fragment of winter range—a very real danger, one must remember, judging by experience with reindeer?

Elsewhere throughout southern Alaska, intensive protection from both wolves and hunting is being extended to the caribou, always on the apparent assumption that the range will carry the increase. Perhaps the Nelchina range and all the others can carry many more animals, in which case the present program of herd increase is entirely justified. But on all these ranges there will come a point when further increase is dangerous. We are deeply concerned with the lack of criteria by which to evaluate this condition and more importantly by the lack of an adequate plan to obtain such information. Field studies of caribou and their ranges, initiated by the Fish and Wildlife Service in 1948, are excellent as far as they go, but the problem is so critical as to warrant considerably more attention in our opinion.

Throughout Alaska there has been an appreciable increase of wolves in the past two decades. No one really knows what caused the increase, though we have wondered if the recent peak population of reindeer might have been a contributory factor, the wolves fattening and increasing on the thousands of strays that roamed western Alaska. After the reindeer crash, the wolves could have drifted east and north where we find them today. Or perhaps this is merely one of those mysterious fluctuations which characterize populations of wild *Canidae* the world over.

Wolves are reported to be on the increase in Canada and Scandinavia as well as in Alaska. Whatever the cause, we seriously doubt that the wolves have played any major role in the decrease of caribou which started far back when wolves were very scarce. On the same range the moose, which is another important prey of the wolf, has been steadily increasing, and the total moose-caribou situation is much more logically explained on the basis of changing range conditions.

The importance of wolves and of wolf predation, therefore, should be viewed as one factor which has served in the past, and may be called upon in the future, to help prevent overpopulations of caribou, and of other large mammals as well. Regulating wolf numbers can be a delicate tool in regulating caribou numbers. But like other tools of management, the control of wolf predation should be an integrated part of a total program. Deer irruptions all over the United States attest to the fallacy of closely regulating hunting and predation without reference to range limitations.

Caribou north of the Arctic Circle

Whereas from the facts at hand there can be no doubt of the decrease of caribou in central and southern Alaska, we are of the belief that caribou in the north are at least as numerous as they were fifty years ago and perhaps even more so.

In the era from 1900 to about 1925, many explorers and investigators crossed and recrossed the Brooks Range and the Arctic prairie, and their journals collectively constitute a reliable record of game conditions at that time. Some of the most valuable of these are accounts by Stefansson

(1913), Schrader (1900 and 1904), Leffingwell (1919), Smith and Mertie (1930), and Mertie (1930). When one reads these journals and compares the numbers of caribou seen then with herds observed in recent years, there appears to have been a substantial increase.

Stefansson spent two years in extreme northeastern Alaska and adjoining northwestern Canada and complained of the great scarcity of caribou. He indicated that the decrease (from some previous high) had caused a substantial decrease in the Eskimo population. Herds of 7,500 to 10,000 are known in this area today, in fact one such herd passed our camp site at Schrader Lake.

Smith and Mertie say that there were only scattered, small bands of caribou in the Colville drainage and practically none in the Noatak drainage, where now herds estimated from 7,000 to 100,000 occur (Scott *et al.*, 1950, and Table 3).

Leffingwell (1919) records a material decrease in caribou numbers along the international boundary from 1907 to 1912, blaming it on native hunting. In 1911–12 and again in 1913–14 he could obtain practically no caribou for food. But in 1950, Scott and associates list the Chandalar herd as 20,000. In 1949 Marston Beaver of Fort Yukon was camped near the Firth River just west of the boundary and he states that a large herd migrated past his camp for four days and nights, headed southeast.

Many of the above cases of apparent changes in caribou abundance could be due merely to shifts in location of big herds. It is suggested in fact that the Yukon-Tanana herd may have moved north across the Yukon River, thereby accounting for the sudden increase in northern caribou populations. But the point we are making is that in the north there seem to be fully as many big bands now as there were half a century ago, if not more.

The intensive pursuit of caribou by Eskimos has all but ceased over most of northern Alaska, which factor may have furthered the recovery in numbers. Only around Anaktuvuk Pass (Rausch, 1951) and near the coastal villages are caribou still hunted on the Arctic slope; even there the Nunamiut Eskimos reported to Rausch that caribou had increased. Most Eskimos now work for wages and are less dependent upon caribou for food and clothing.

The truly Arctic tundra does not burn and has only locally been grazed by reindeer, so the range is probably as good as it ever was. But in our view, it appears to be relatively poor winter range for caribou, lichens being sparse at best and very slow to recover from grazing. Likewise Banfield (1951) found winter densities of caribou very low along the Arctic coast of Canada. Most of the large herds visit the Arctic slope in spring, summer, and fall, but midwinter usually is spent on better lichen ranges to the south, in the edge of the taiga. Regular migrations are noted through Anaktuvuk Pass and we suspect they occur as well through many other passes in the Brooks Range.

If the northern caribou ranges are in fact inferior in carrying capacity, numbers now being quite high and hunting pressure low, there is, it seems to us, an incipient danger of overpopulation and range damage. A recent intensive drive against wolves in the region around Umiat resulted in elimination of over 250 animals by shooting and poisoning, for the avowed purpose of protecting caribou. In the same area natives normally bounty around 100 additional wolves per year. Again we raise the question whether this intensity of control should not be preceded by at least a cursory survey to ascertain whether the range can carry the expected increase in caribou numbers. We further question whether this particular operation is in line with the avowed policy of the Fish and Wildlife Service, as set forth by Presnall (1950), to permit predators and prey to seek their own balance in wilderness areas where hunting is removing less than the annual increment in the prey populations.

Research needs

Repeatedly we have had to point out how little is known about caribou and their range requirements. Perhaps the biggest problem of all is the initiation of research to learn how to manage the animals and their ranges before serious mistakes are made which could greatly complicate the present situation.

In our view, caribou investigations should take two forms. First, the aerial surveys of caribou numbers, so well started by the Fish and Wildlife Service, should be expanded to include ground surveys of range conditions. In fact, two competent biologists, with an airplane, might well be detailed to undertake a full-fledged investigation of caribou and their ranges throughout the Territory, such as was conducted in Canada by Banfield (1951) and his assistants. Within a short period, results from such a general study could be put to use in determining desirable hunting regulations, predator control policy, areas needing high priority in fire control, and other matters of immediate concern to management.

However, short-term undertakings of the sort described above will not of themselves yield a substantial accumulation of information on the natural history and ecology of

PLATE 1a. Arrival at Mekoryuk on Nunivak Island in Bering Sea.

PLATE 1b. Village of Mekoryuk (population 155) showing reindeer corral, slaughterhouse, and overhead rail to beach.

Plate 2. Reindeer bulls in shallows, Nunivak Island.

PLATE 3. Caribou bulls escaping mosquitoes by wading into the shallows of the Arctic Ocean, near the mouth of the Colville River. The northward summer migration across the Arctic plain is made up largely of male animals, most of the females and calves of northern herds summering in the Brooks Range. The kill by Eskimo hunters consists largely of bulls, hence is not a serious drain on caribou populations.

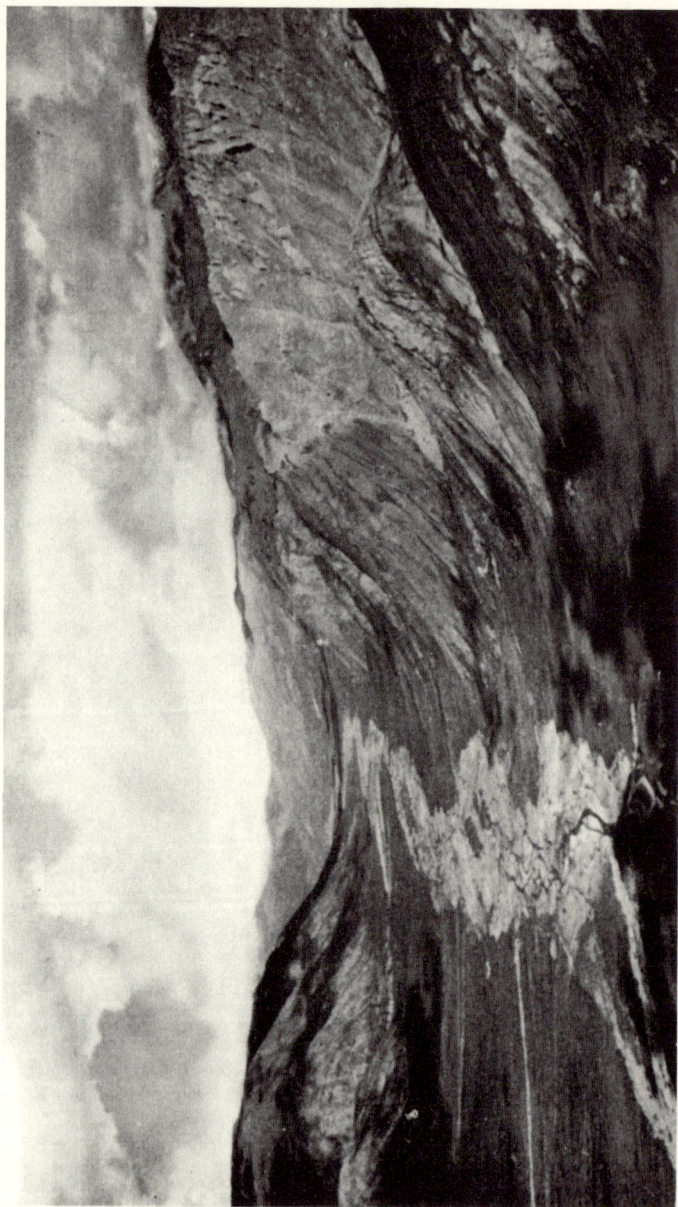

PLATE 4. Looking northward along the Hulahula River in the Romanzof Mountains, Arctic slope of the Brooks Range. The typically U-shaped glaciated valleys in this area are frequented by large bands of caribou in summer, but are poor winter range. Dall sheep occupy the mountains.

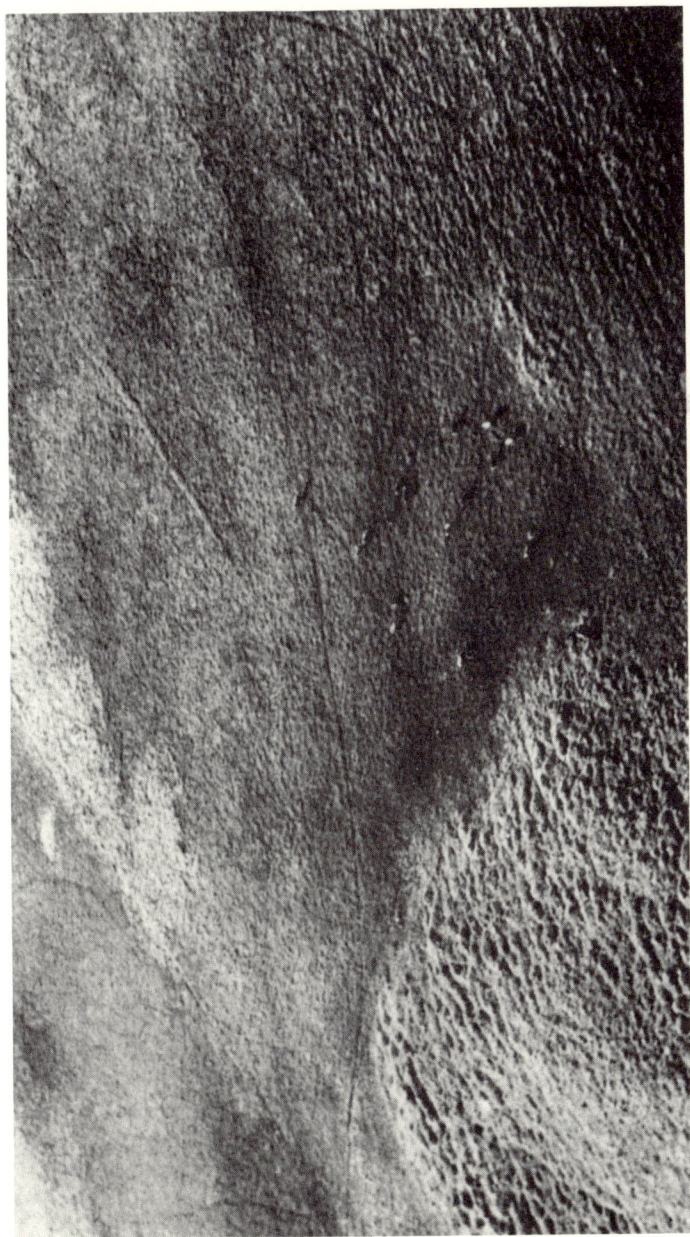

Plate 5. Trails of caribou herds on the Alaska Peninsula. A few animals are visible. (E. P. Haddon, U.S. Fish and Wildlife Service)

PLATE 6. Branching lichens are staple winter food for caribou. (D. L. Spencer, U.S. Fish and Wildlife Service)

PLATE 7a. Heavy growth of lichens (genus *Cladonia*) among spruce trees on an island in Lake Tustumena, Kenai Peninsula. In the Kenai area such growths persist only on islands, since nearly all the mainland has burned. (D. L. Spencer, U.S. Fish and Wildlife Service)

PLATE 7b. Approximately 30 years after a burn, the spruces are just beginning to emerge from the mat of sedge, grass, and willow. It will be many years before the branching lichens reinvade. Scene near Steese Highway east of Fairbanks.

PLATE 8a. Fire burning through taiga range near Dillingham, north of Bristol Bay. Such fires have destroyed 80 per cent of the caribou winter range in central and southern Alaska.

PLATE 8b. Winter range of the Nelchina caribou herd in the upper Susitna drainage. This is one of the few unburned areas of taiga in southern Alaska.

PLATE 9. Heavily browsed willows on winter moose range near Kasilof, Kenai Peninsula. The shrubs are still sprouting, despite being mowed off to snow line each winter.

PLATE 10a. Yukon River near Circle, Alaska, showing process of erosion and redeposition of bars. Willows colonize the new silt beds. In this manner good moose range is maintained perpetually.

PLATE 10b. Part of the Yukon-Kuskokwim delta plain opposite Nunivak Island. The 22,000 square miles of wet tundra between the mouths of the Yukon and Kuskokwim rivers is a major breeding ground for North American waterfowl, especially geese and brant.

PLATE 11a. Fish wheel in the Yukon River, near Fort Yukon. Salmon taken in various kinds of nets and traps are an important item of diet for native peoples and their sled dogs.

PLATE 11b. Seal skins curing on racks at Nash Harbor, Nunivak Island, will be used to cover the kayak frames shown in the background.

PLATE 12. An Eskimo approaches the edge of the Bering Sea ice field, where he will use the kayak, now resting on its sled, to hunt seals. As he approaches the water, he tests the thickness of the ice with his spear. (Machetanz, Shostal)

PLATE 13. Sheefish on drying racks, Kotzebue. Establishment of permanent Eskimo villages, in place of the easily moved camps of the past, has created serious problems of water supply and general sanitation.

Plate 14a. Removal of overburden from gold-bearing sands with high pressure hoses, at Ester.

Plate 14b. A gold dredge in action on the Yukon.

PLATE 15. Muskox herd in Nunivak Wildlife Refuge. (D. L. Spencer, U.S. Fish and Wildlife Service)

PLATE 16. Sunrise Glacier, Mt. McKinley Park. Alaska is generously endowed with superb scenery. (Machetanz, Shostal)

the caribou, without which we can never fully understand this elusive and enigmatic animal. Someone must settle down to the tedious task of studying the caribou in its entire life cycle and in its specific relations to the flora and to other animals. Preferably this should be done in an isolated situation with a minimum of interference by changing patterns of hunting and of land use. The great wilderness of the eastern Brooks Range, recommended elsewhere in this report for preservation as an Arctic wilderness, would be an ideal place to conduct such a study. There would be enormous difficulties to overcome in such an undertaking (that is perhaps the reason no one has yet started). Merely keeping up with the herds is a problem of considerable complication. But the need is great, and the expenditure of funds and effort could well be justified in terms of the importance of the species.

Summary

Caribou have been eliminated from western Alaska by reindeer grazing and very much reduced in central and southern Alaska by burning over the winter range. Only north of the Arctic Circle is the range more or less intact, and there caribou seem to be as abundant as they ever were.

On the basis of this situation, we postulate that the big problem in caribou management is preservation of the range and not control of decimating factors, such as hunting and predation, which have been getting most of the attention.

To arrive at a satisfactory solution of the problems of caribou management much more study is needed, both of the animals and of their ranges.

6

THE STATUS OF THE REINDEER

The early Russian occupation of Alaska was concerned almost wholly with fur resources. The second half of the nineteenth century witnessed a change in slant to oil and baleen obtained from whales, and oil and ivory from walruses, the ships coming through the Bering Straits from the Pacific, rounding Point Barrow and reaching as far as Herschel Island west of the Mackenzie Delta. These ships sought directly for export profit a resource hunted by the Eskimo, and in order to help sustain the crews, inroads were made on any game to be found near the west and north coasts of Alaska. Game was also attacked from the landward when mining was begun on the Seward Peninsula. The result of such depletion of resources, for the sustenance of what was little less than a marauding population, was that the resident Eskimos were reduced to starvation and many hundreds perished as a result of absence of game and from diseases introduced by the white man.

Growth and decline of the reindeer population

Doctor Sheldon Jackson, a missionary and later United States General Agent for Education in Alaska, conceived the idea of replacing the depleted animals of seas and coasts in the economy of the Eskimo by reindeer which could subsist on the landward ranges. Jackson's pertinacity brought about the importation from Siberia of 16 reindeer (*Rangifer tarandus*) in 1891 and 171 in 1892. Between 1891 and 1902 a total of 1,280 reindeer were imported.

TABLE 5. A record of the increase and crash of reindeer in Alaska, from the time of their introduction to the present

Year	Estimated numbers of reindeer	Authority
1892	143	Reports, Office of U. S. General Agent for Education in Alaska
1895	743	"
1900	2,692	"
1902	4,795	"
1905	10,241	"
1910	27,325	"
1912	38,476	Hanson (1952)
1914	57,872	"
1916	82,151	"
1917	81,086	"
1920	180,000	Reports of U. S. Senate Reindeer Committee
1921	216,000	"
1923	300,000	"
1926	350,000	"
1930	500,000	"
1932	625,000–650,000	Lantis (1950); Hanson (1952)
1936	594,000	Hanson (1952)
1940	252,550	Burdick (1940)
1948	32,623	Alaska Native Service, Juneau
1952	26,735	"

Administration of the reindeer project was carefully ordered. Lapp herders came from Scandinavia to manage the herds and to train Eskimos as herders. The period of apprenticeship was four years. The government, once it accepted responsibility for administration, kept a fairly tight hold on disposal of the deer. Natives were forbidden to sell or slaughter females, and mission and government herds were also conserved on this principle of using only surplus males for meat and skins. Predation on the herds was negligible and a rate of increase approaching reproductive potential seems to have been achieved in many places. Growth of the whole Alaskan population of reindeer is shown in Table 5.

The rapid increase from 1892 to 1932 was dangerous by reason of its success. The first need for which the reindeer were imported, namely, to provide a food reserve for the native people, was soon fulfilled, and numbers were expanding beyond what natives, missions, and the government could handle conveniently. A few white owners came into this new pastoral industry and began to commercialize it for export. As the situation was contrived, with all parties quite agreed that expansion was desirable, a developed commercialization would have been a merciful safety valve preventing overstocking of the range. But the animals reproduced faster than the organization of the new industry, and before long, herding practice had deteriorated, marketing was lax, and frictions developed. The truth would seem to be that the industry with half a million deer in an immense country with only a limited manpower, was out of control.

Then, in the late 1930's, the reindeer began to diminish in number. At first the decline was slight, but losses increased to catastrophic proportions. We have certain valuable statistics of the collapse. First, the political situation ultimately demanded that white ownership of reindeer should cease, and that the government should buy the deer and redistribute them among Alaskan natives (Roberts, 1942). We are in no way concerned with the rights and wrongs of this situation, but as ecologists we are grateful for the extremely careful work of Burdick of the U. S. Forest Service, who was responsible for the negotiations during the change-over. The census in the spring of 1940, after an Act of Congress authorized the Secretary of Interior to purchase all non-native-owned deer and equipment, gave a total of 252,550. At that time the Alaska Native Service took over the management of the deer. By 1941 the numbers had dropped to 155,000, counted from 42 roundups. The numbers in 1948 were 32,623, in 1949, 27,920 and in 1950, 25,000. Numbers have begun now to rise slowly and the figure for 1952 supplied to us by the Alaska Native Service is 26,735, distributed in 15 herds as shown in Table 6 and Figure 3.

TABLE 6. Reindeer herds in Alaska, according to the 1952 annual report of the Alaska Native Service

Name of herd	Estimated size of herd	Location	Ownership
Escholtz Bay	4,300	Kotzebue	Government
York Wilson-Henry Weber	450	Kotzebue	Private
Charlie Smith	600	Selawick	Private
Ross Stalker	975	Noatak	Private
St. Michael	2,100	St. Michael	Government
Sigfried Aukongak	1,700	Golovin	Private
Andrew Skin	1,100	Selawick	Private
Johnny Kakaruk	575	Mary's Igloo	Private
Charlie Clark	1,100	Deering	Private
St. Lawrence Island.....	300	St. Lawrence Island	St. Lawrence Island Association
Nunivak Island	5,500	Nunivak Island	Government
Atka Island	3,500	Atka Island	Government
Umnak Island	1,500	Umnak Island	Government
Alitak	3,000	Kodiak Island	Private
Pribilof	35	St. Paul Island	Government, under the supervision of the Fish and Wildlife Service
	26,735 head (1952 calves included)		

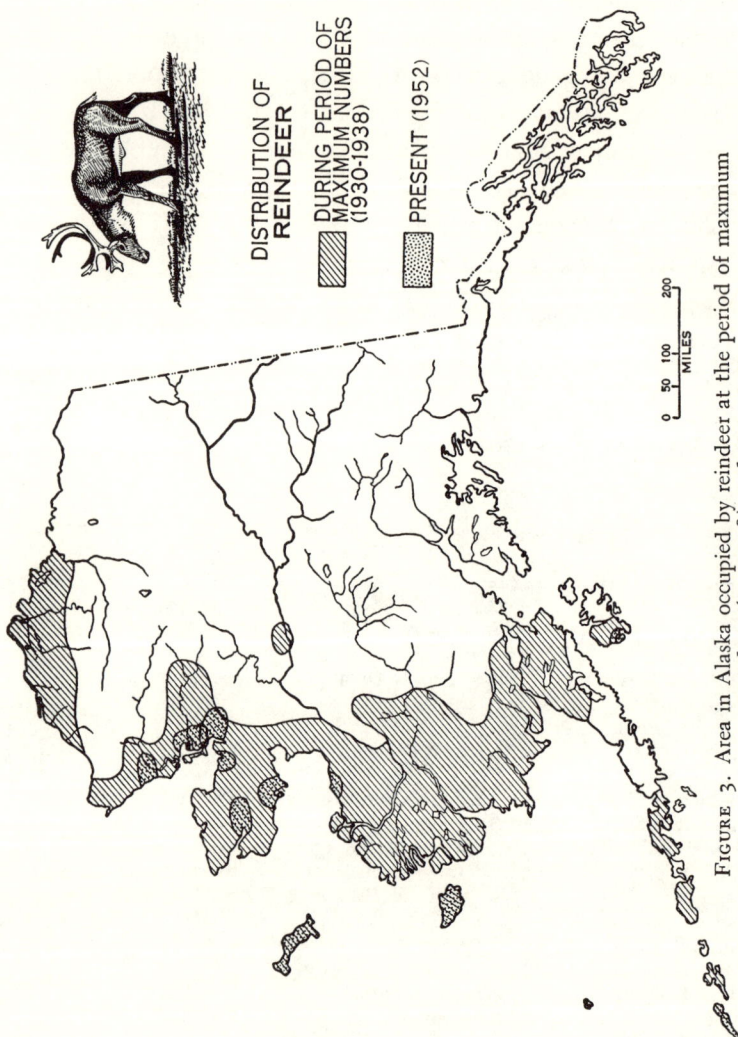

FIGURE 3. Area in Alaska occupied by reindeer at the period of maximum numbers (1930–38) and at present.

Naturally the collapse of the herd was followed by reports which tried to explain what had happened. Collectively these documents stress the following influences: (*a*) careless herding, resulting in loss of large numbers of strays, including many that were drawn off by passing caribou herds; (*b*) predation by wolves; and (*c*) excessive slaughtering. The same causes of decline are reiterated in the recent retrospective summary of the situation by Lantis (1950). Relatively little attention has been paid to the fact that a major change in the lichen ranges was wrought by the reindeer themselves.

Winter range relationships

We would suggest that the rise and fall of the reindeer population in Alaska is an example on a grand scale, and well documented, of the typical swarming and crashing of an animal population suffering but few checks. It is regrettable that a population of ungulates can graze or browse more than the annual increment on its range and still go on increasing and apparently thriving. The stockman tends to see the animals only and remains content if they increase and thrive. But the condition of the range, and particularly of the winter range, is the crucial matter in the management of ungulate populations, and the ecologist is only now training himself to analyze and correctly assess range condition. L. J. Palmer, who worked so long and well on the agronomy of reindeer pastoralism, recognized the situation too late to prevent the crash. Indeed, the increase of the herds was like a flood, and he could not possibly have stemmed the catastrophe during the last years of increase.

Study of the Alaskan reindeer ranges, principally by Palmer (1945), had been in progress from 1920 on, but the early estimates of carrying capacities were much too optimistic. In this western coastal country which for some years had certainly not been fully utilized by caribou, grazing potential appeared to be very high. Lichen ranges, unlike grass or browse ranges, "stockpile" unused forage, hence look better every year. The Senate Reindeer Committee of 1931 had before it a computation from the Reindeer Research Station, that 954,800 deer could be pastured between Seward Peninsula and the lower Kuskokwim, by no means the full extent of considered reindeer range. The Seward Peninsula, of 12,880,528 acres, was computed to have a grazing capacity of 202,000 deer—one deer to 64 acres, or ten to a square mile. With such figures in hand, it did not seem possible that the reindeer might be overgrazing their range. Hence when the crash came, factors other than range were blamed.

As evidence of the fact that the rise and fall of reindeer was in fact a range phenomenon, and not owing primarily to the loss of strays, to wolf predation, or to poaching, we cite the situation on various islands where none of the latter influences applied. On Nunivak, St. Lawrence, and St. Paul islands where there were no wolves, no caribou with which the reindeer might run away, and where the killing by native people was very limited, the herds built up and crashed in precisely the same way as on the mainland. Scheffer (1951) has documented completely the story of reindeer on St. Paul Island. We can add here a brief account of what happened on Nunivak Island.

Caribou became extinct on Nunivak about 1870. There were no grazing animals on the island then until 1920 when the Lomen Reindeer Corporation landed 99 reindeer. These increased to 2,500 by 1931 and to 17,000 by 1940. The animals apparently numbered 22,000 in the mid-1940's and the population began to crash in 1946. Colonization of the island had been made later than elsewhere, and the collapse was ten years later. The situation was grasped to some extent, in that 13,000 carcasses were shipped out in the period 1945–47, but such assisted reduction was insufficient to stop collapse, which came in the hard winter of 1948. The government is now aiming to keep the Nunivak herd at around 5,000, and at this figure some 1,000 carcasses a year are being shipped out.

Our examination of the island shows that the nutritious and palatable lichens have been largely eliminated. Their regeneration may take half a century, a century, or some indefinite period much longer than that. Nunivak Island shows the interesting phenomenon of the surviving reindeer having now gone over to a diet which is predominately willow, most of the *Cladonia* having been grazed out. The low willow bushes show heavy scarring from the 1940's, but they are now recovering. Whether the range will sustain the deer through very severe winters is not yet known. The present productivity in the herd, 20 per cent per year, is much less than the 33 per cent which Hadwen (1939) states is normal for herds situated on good lichen ranges.

The situation on the west coast, typified by Seward Peninsula, and the Baldwin Peninsula near Kotzebue, is particularly interesting. When the reindeer first came, there was an abundant climax lichen cover. The influx of miners caused numerous tundra fires. Such fires can occur only when there is an abundance of lichens. As we know, the reindeer grazed out the remainder of the lichen cover. It is usual to think of overgrazing as producing desert conditions, but on the reindeer ranges the result has been the creation of a great coastal expanse of summer range consisting of a lush growth of sedges and shrubs, such as *Eriophorum* (cotton sedge), grasses such as *Calamagrostis* and *Festuca rubra,* dwarf birch, willows and Labrador tea (*Ledum*). One of Palmer's quadrats situated eight miles northeast of Nome, and described by him in 1922, had at that time a ground cover of 90–92 per cent lichens 4 inches high. The lichens had been reduced to 75 per cent, and 3–4 inches in height, in 1928. Hanson described this plot again in 1951, when it contained blueberry (*Vaccinium*), crowberry (*Empetrum*), heather (*Cassiope*), etc., and only a sparse lichen cover. The change is directly attributable to reindeer grazing. Our opinion is that where this change to a dense lush herbage has taken place, lichen regeneration is unlikely in the foreseeable future. Where the lichen is regenerating, it is on the harder types of ground, and here it is making good progress.

Herding problems and native attitudes

It is reasonably certain that in addition to sheer numbers of reindeer, overgrazing was aggravated by methods, or lack of methods, of herding. On tender or easily upset plant associations, successful pastoralism in terms of conservation of habitat depends upon adoption of a nomadic culture, as typified, for example, by the Lapps and Tartars. Wherever a more or less sedentary pastoralism has been practiced on a marginal habitat, as in Australia, South Africa, and the western United States, deterioration of the habitat has occurred. The Arctic and sub-Arctic grazing grounds can be just as arid for a large part of the year through frost action as are those mentioned above through actual lack of precipitation. The nomadic behavior of the caribou, described elsewhere in this report, doubtless conforms to what the habitat demands—swift movement and only occasional usage.

The Lapp in Scandinavia has conserved his habitat for reindeer grazing and he accepts the necessity for movement with his animals. There is considerable literature on the Lapp methods of herding and of rotating winter pastures— methods that were worked out empirically over centuries of time and have been described by Scandinavian ecologists in relatively recent years. Thus the accounts of Aaltonen (1919) in Finland and of Rowell (1922) and Lynge (1921) in Norway are classics in the field. A recent paper by Hustich (1951) summarizes in English both the European and North American literature on the subject. The need for rotating reindeer grazing on lichen ranges is almost universally recognized, and Hustich cites the following estimates of time required for lichens to recover from one passage of a reindeer herd: "3–7 years (Lönnberg, 1909); 6–15 years (Itkonen, 1948); 10–20 up to 40 years (Lynge, 1921); 15–20 years (Räsänen, 1928); 15–30 years (Tengvall, 1928)." These are the estimated periods, in other words, during which ranges should be left ungrazed so that they can recover. Manifestly, herds must be moved far and often to avoid passing a given locality more often than once in ten years, which is Hustich's suggested average interval between grazings.

It would seem that neither Eskimo herders nor most of the whites (excepting the transported Lapps) were mobile enough to follow any such grazing schedule. Attachments for home camps or villages apparently led to repeated graz-

ing of the coastal ranges and their ultimate exhaustion.
We have wondered why the Eskimo should not easily become a reindeer nomad, because as a people they are involved in much movement in their hunting and visiting.
Possibly the movement of following the herds or guiding
their travel is incompatible with the Eskimo's motivation
to movement which is interception of caribou, of walrus,
or of seals on their passage. We do not know.

We received interesting insight into this fundamental
difference in outlook on pastoral movement in talking with
a Fisheries Officer who had been encamped with his col-
leagues throughout the summer of 1930 on the Egegik
River on the Alaska Peninsula. He said that Alaskan natives (Eskimo-Aleut) who owned reindeer herds on the
Peninsula would bring them meat twice a week regularly
from some place not far distant where they were camped
with their herd, apparently for the summer. A Lapp owner
would also sell meat to them, but only if he happened to
be passing their way with his herd. To the Lapp, the movement of his herd was more important than a ready market.

Coming now to the charges that poor husbandry by Eskimo herders and predation by wolves led to the loss of
large numbers of reindeer, these cannot be denied. Unless
constantly tended, reindeer herds often scatter and the
strays are easily run down by wolves. The present effort of
the Alaska Native Service to train thoroughly the men en-
trusted with herds and to supervise their work is entirely
necessary. So also is the control of wolves on primary reindeer ranges, though good herding tends to minimize predation losses. In stressing the range situation we do not mean
to overlook the importance of good husbandry. This need
was stressed by H. C. Hanson (1952) who recently studied

the present outlook for reindeer pastoralism on behalf of the Alaska Native Service. Coming from such a distinguished botanist and agricultural ecologist, one of his conclusions is of particular interest, namely, that whatever the pastoral possibilities, the industry should revive now only as good, tried herders are found. The problem, then, is not solely botanical, but one of human ecology.

This is a point at which we may well discuss the Eskimo's attitude to wealth and how little he really understands the money values of our society. The Eskimo's environment and his capacity for mobility—which does not conflict with his sociability and his habit of making more or less permanent villages in Alaska—has produced a race which does not encumber itself with masses of permanent wealth. Accumulation of things would mean logistic problems with which the Eskimo does not wish to burden himself. The primitive Eskimo, who thinks not of the morrow and thus remains happy and smiling in circumstances which would engender neuroses in the white man, has wealth in his skills, in his successful hunting methods, and in producing necessary artifacts. He can use his wealth to gain prestige by ceremonial acts of giving away to less fortunate persons. He does not accumulate.

If this is his pristine philosophy, the possession of wealth as dollars or reindeer can have little true meaning for him. The dollars are often squandered in buying flashy radios, typewriters, tennis shoes, and what not; the reindeer may be a millstone around his neck, depriving him of sociability and subjecting him to a pattern of movement dictated by the needs of the deer. We have been told at first hand of an Eskimo who owned a large herd of reindeer within the last three years. The young men who were tending them during his occasional absence lost four-fifths of the herd, a great loss by our standards. This Eskimo laughed: here was a joke he could crack for the rest of his life—that those boys had lost most of his deer while he was away on a visit. He still had left, in one-fifth of the herd, far more reindeer than he could use in the immediate future or even during some considerable time. As that Eskimo's life will be lived, he is probably quite right; he has not lost anything that would have made him any more comfortable. He can afford the cost of the fine perennial joke, and indeed, it may be looked upon as his way of using wealth.

If the Eskimo is to take our values and our culture, he must be educated to our notions of wealth and its proper use, but we see few signs of such tutelage. We know of one large business house in the Territory, employing a great deal of Eskimo labor, that has persuaded the Eskimos to buy grub stakes in the fall, to the amount of $1,000 and more, so that the family shall be well fed until the end of winter; some banking is also done by the company on the Eskimos' behalf. There should be more of this type of guidance. It is not suggested that the Native Service can interfere with a native's free choice, but there can be help, advice, and education using anthropological insight. It is altogether too much to subject a race in a primitive stage of material culture to the high-pressure barrage of the most complex technological and commercial civilization the world has ever known, and expect the Eskimo to display great prudence and forethought.

Finally, we think the North American attitude to wealth and business usage might well be laid aside in the administration of the reindeer industry by the Alaska Native Service. As it is, an Eskimo can borrow 500 reindeer from the government but he must pay back the 500 deer in five years' time. In effect, reindeer husbandry is being run on the gold standard; the indebted Eskimo endures the Domoclean reckoning over his head and the government receives back deer it does not want. The first real value of reindeer to an Eskimo is that he should eat them and ward off starvation and sickness. If the industry goes off the "gold standard," there will be greater fluidity and the government should soon be able to shed responsibility for herds of reindeer it does not wish to own. There will always remain, however, continuing responsibility for technical guidance which the government must supply. It was lack of such guidance that brought the reindeer industry to its present unhappy state.

Summary

The reindeer population thrived and grew on the rich climax growth of lichens that covered western Alaska half a century ago. As a result of overgrazing, and locally of burning, we now have a changed botanical complex and one which does not sustain the deer in winter time. The immense area of summer range which has been created cannot be utilized because the remaining winter lichen ranges are too far inland. This change in the herbage complex is, in our opinion, the overwhelming cause of the collapse of the reindeer population, with predation, lapses in herding, and straying to caribou herds as minor contributing factors.

The outlook for reindeer grazing as a major Alaskan industry would appear to be dim. The success of the first 40 years carried the germs of its own failure, and as a history it is one more example of the need for preliminary as well as coincident ecological research in land use in any new country. Reindeer husbandry now can probably do exactly what it was originally intended to do, namely, help to provide a reasonable diet of protein for the native Eskimo of Alaska. The depleted ranges of the present time must continue to be only lightly stocked for many years to come. Studies of the lichen flora should be reactivated and put on a year-round basis by a crew of trained range technicians who can help the Alaska Native Service to control and direct grazing practice as the herds slowly rebuild.

7

THE STATUS OF THE MOOSE

THE MAGNIFICENT moose of Alaska (*Alces americana*) has long been recognized as the largest in the world. In the late nineteenth century, a good many wealthy European and American sportsmen started coming to southern Alaska, especially to the Kenai Peninsula, seeking record heads; the stream of trophy hunters has not diminished even to the present day. Next to the giant brown bear, the moose is Alaska's most famed hunting trophy.

Of more real significance, however, has been the continuing importance of the moose as a source of meat for both natives and whites in central and southern Alaska. The Russian fur traders who settled in the vicinity of Cook Inlet obtained many moose as well as caribou from the Kenaitze Indians to sustain their settlements, and Lieutenant Schwatka who first mapped the whole length of the Yukon River speaks in his diary (1885) of the dependence of both Indians and white traders on moose for fresh meat. During the trapping-prospecting period of the early part of this century, the moose was the mainstay for literally thousands of settlers wintering in isolated cabins over much of Alaska. Probably during that era hunting pressure reached its peak, and numbers of moose in turn reached so low an

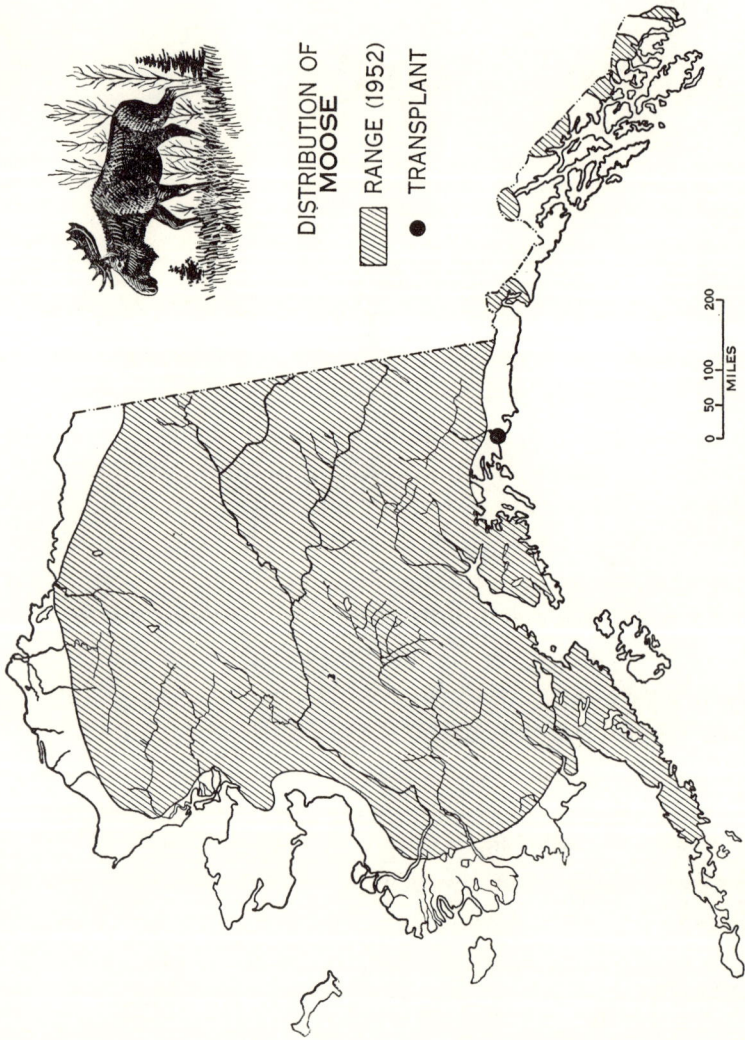

DISTRIBUTION OF
MOOSE

RANGE (1952)

● TRANSPLANT

0 50 100   200
        MILES

FIGURE 4. The present distribution of moose in Alaska. The range is now more extensive than it was fifty years ago and local densities are higher.

ebb as to cause concern for the future of the species. In recent years, with the imposition of hunting restrictions, moose have recovered their numbers and in some areas at least have attained densities that perhaps never were achieved before. Furthermore, they have extended their range northward and westward into areas where formerly they were absent or at least very scarce. Figure 4 shows the present range of moose in Alaska. It is necessary to consider the ecologic affinities of the moose to understand its present abundance.

Browse ranges needed by moose

Completely unlike the caribou, the moose over most of its range is dependent upon a subclimax type of vegetation. When a spruce forest is burned or cut, the first woody plants to invade are normally willow, aspen, or birch. These tend to dominate the vegetation for a period of years during which the slow-growing spruce regenerates. Eventually the hardwoods die out and mature spruce once again forms the climax forest. It is during the period when the willow, aspen, and birch are young that moose thrive best, for these three plants furnish the bulk of the browse on which moose winter. And ordinarily it is the supply of winter food that determines the moose population.

Previous mention has been made of the extensive burns in the spruce lands of southern and central Alaska. The very fires which eliminated lichen range for caribou created tremendous areas of good browse range for moose. In our flights over the former spruce lands we noted repeatedly the existence of secondary growths of hardwoods in old burns. Particularly on the Kenai Peninsula and in the lower Susitna drainage, uncounted fires have maintained large acreages in browse stages satisfactory for moose to winter. In these areas winter densities up to 50 animals per square mile are found.

In recent years moose have been increasing in number and spreading their range on the Alaska Peninsula. Near Mother Goose Lake, for example, we saw a number of moose from the air and sign was abundant on the ground. This area is at present well grown with young stands of aspen and cottonwood now in the pole or sapling stage, and three kinds of willow, on which the animals are wintering. We presume that this growth came in following a fire, or series of fires, a decade or two ago. A limited open season on moose will be held on the Peninsula this year, where in the recent past moose were scarcely known (Osgood, 1901).

Most of the Yukon drainage, including the main tributaries, likewise has burned over, and one can fly for hours over fine moose range in various stages of second growth. Moose are not uniformly abundant in central Alaska, however, for reasons that are not entirely clear to us. Local overhunting, particularly in the vicinity of Indian villages, certainly is one factor. But some areas rather remote from settlements do not carry as many moose as the range appears capable of supporting. The status of this important animal in central Alaska is worthy of careful study. Most moose studies in Alaska to date have been conducted on the southern ranges, near Cook Inlet.

On the alluvial plains of the larger rivers, large areas of willow are maintained by natural processes other than fire. Along the Yukon, between Fort Yukon and Circle for example, one can see clearly the constant effects of erosion and deposition of silt upon plant succession. The multiple channels of the river are continuously cutting away at high banks, which are generally grown over with mature willow and birch, and are depositing new bars on which young willows colonize. This results in the maintenance of young browse stands in just the proper stage of growth to supply the needs of moose. It is easy to understand why moose have always thrived along the river bottoms.

On the northern and western fringes of the Alaskan moose range, willow is not a secondary plant invader but rather it is part of the riparian climax vegetation, the uplands being tundra. The factor which governs the abundance of willow here is not fire, as in the central and southern spruce forests, but probably temperature. We postulate that the recent spread of moose into predominantly tundra areas must be correlated with the gradual Holarctic warming that is known to have occurred in the past half century.

Although Rausch (1951) and others have pointed out that at least a few moose have been known to exist on the Arctic slope for many years, there is a considerable body of evidence that the species is both extending its northern range and increasing in numbers. Along the Colville River, for example, moose are now abundant; from an airplane one can see a dozen animals easily within a few miles of Umiat, tracks on the ground are everywhere to be seen, and the willows are heavily browsed. Yet neither Schrader (1904), Leffingwell (1919) nor Smith and Mertie (1930) even mention the species in recounting their travels along the Colville River in the first decades of this century.

Likewise we noted moose droppings on the ridge just east of Schrader Lake, at least 75 miles from any previously known moose range. James Brooks of the University of

Alaska in 1949 saw a moose on Cape Prince of Wales over 100 miles west of the nearest known range. Stefansson (1913) commented upon the recent increase of moose near Bear Lake in northern Canada; he stated that in 1909 the first moose was seen on Coronation Gulf near the mouth of Coppermine River. Anderson (1924) further elaborated upon the northward spread in Canada. Kalela (1948, 1949) and Siivonen (1952) in Finland have written at length about the northward shift of a number of vertebrates, including roe deer, which phenomenon they ascribe to temperature change.

Presumably the gradual warming has permitted an extension of the range of tall willows (a *primary* step in succession, rather than secondary as when willow invades burned forest), which in turn permits the moose to winter farther north. Dr. J. L. Giddings, Jr., of the University of Pennsylvania, who has been measuring tree ring growth in the Arctic, tells us that for fifty years past the rings have been getting progressively wider, a fact which would seem to substantiate the presumed improvement in growing conditions for woody plants with the rising temperatures.

In southern Alaska, moose recently have invaded some new range in the Taku River drainage, apparently as a result of the melting away of a glacier which had acted as a barrier. Moose have been introduced into the delta of the Copper River, another area insulated by glaciers from surrounding moose range.

Whereas in the north and west, management of browse ranges must be limited to regulating their use, as will be discussed presently, we foresee the possibility of deliberately creating moose range in the spruce zone by manipulating plant successions.

The wildfires of the past inadvertently improved many Alaskan ranges for moose at an exorbitant cost in timber, watershed cover, and caribou range. It is unthinkable that we can permit unregulated burning to continue. The ambitious but sadly underfinanced fire control program of the Bureau of Land Management (Division of Forestry) is the first positive step to curb this destruction. Assuming that wildfire can be arrested in the future, there remains the opportunity for the *controlled* use of fire to improve selected winter ranges for moose where other values may be considered subservient.

On key areas for moose, such as wintering ground on the Kenai National Moose Range, experiments might well be started at once to learn when, how, and if small fires, deliberately set, might be used to perpetuate willow and birch reproduction for moose forage.

The mere passage of a fire through timberland does not necessarily create optimum conditions for moose. Some burns produce a grassland stage; others come back in pure spruce; many produce aspen with little birch or willow, which are the most palatable and productive browse plants. It may take many years of careful and expensive work merely to learn how fire can be used in moose management and what are its limitations.

But if the moose is destined to be as important as we think it will be in future Alaskan economy, this effort and expense is negligible.

Regulation of hunting

As mentioned above, overhunting of moose was nearly universal a few decades back, but so effective has been the protective program of the Fish and Wildlife Service that many Alaskan ranges now appear to us to be stocked to capacity or locally beyond capacity, the principal exceptions being around Indian settlements in the Yukon valley. The main problem of managing moose now seems to be evaluating present populations in relation to range capacities and maintaining an optimum breeding density *while harvesting the full annual surplus.*

Examination of moose winter ranges on the Kenai Peninsula in company with David L. Spencer, and in the Matanuska Valley with Robert Scott and Edward Chatelain, thoroughly convinced us that at least these populations are being underharvested. Most of the young willow, birch, and aspen in both areas had been mowed off to the snowline by moose each winter and in fact much of the browse, especially aspen, had been killed. In late winter when available browse was all eaten, the moose had taken to scraping bark off larger trees, or in some areas had started eating alder—an unpalatable food of low nutritive value. The range looked much worse on the Kenai than in Matanuska. As in the case of caribou, we are in no way able to say what constitutes optimum range use by moose, but what we saw looked to be used far beyond optimum. It is true that the browsing of moose on willow and birch keeps the plants from growing out of reach and causes subsequent sprouting at low levels, a beneficial effect that we well recognize (Leopold, 1951). But pruning beyond a certain intensity weakens the browse, and overly severe competition for winter food likewise weakens the moose. The low calf crop noted on the Kenai (23 calves: 100 ♀ ♀) is very likely due at least in part to overpopulation and underharvest. The Matanuska range is less heavily used and the calf crop is materially better (61 calves: 100 ♀ ♀).

Present moose-hunting regulations permit the killing of bull moose only. Furthermore, stringent restrictions on when, where, and how a bull may be taken keep the kill down to a negligible part of the population. According to Fish and Wildlife Service estimates, 3,900 legal moose were taken in Alaska in 1950–51. No one knows what the total population may be, but on the basis of sex ratio counts taken on the Kenai (69♂♂ : 100♀♀) and in the Matanuska Valley (63♂♂ : 100♀♀) the kill could hardly represent more than 5 per cent of the population, even allowing for cripples. A higher kill of bulls would cause more distortion of the sex ratio. Since deer herds are known to produce an optimum yield when 25 to 35 per cent of the fall population is harvested, it seems likely that a kill of at least 15 or perhaps 20 per cent of the moose herd would be tolerable. This is one of those questions about Alaskan big game for which no one presently has an answer.

To take even 15 per cent of the moose from fully stocked ranges will require a limited kill of antlerless animals as well as bulls. No experiments in either-sex hunting of moose have been tried in Alaska. Yet in Scandinavia, where moose have been managed successfully for centuries, it is considered essential to harvest part of the cows. Skuncke (1949), as quoted by Peterson (1952) states: ". . . where there is a closed season on cows the number of bulls shot decreases, at times, by as much as 50 per cent of normal. . . . This practice has little in common with true moose conservation."

In short, we question whether adequate use is being made of the moose crop in southern Alaska, where incidentally, the demand for hunting privileges and for meat is highest.

Both the Kenai and the Matanuska-lower Susitna areas are easily accessible by automobile from Anchorage. Wise use of the moose as a resource in this area should strive for maximum allowable harvest rather than deliberate under-harvest, as now seems to be the case.

It must be said that overpopulations of moose do not inevitably lead to violent die-offs or to semipermanent range destruction as occur among deer, reindeer, and perhaps caribou. Individual moose are so hardy that they apparently can make it through a normal winter somehow, even on the poorest kinds of foods, after the better browse is eaten. Extremely severe winters may cause major die-offs, as occurred on the Kenai in 1916, 1923, 1936, and 1946 (Culver, 1923, and D. L. Spencer, personal communication) and along the Yukon in or about the year 1880 according to Schwatka (1885:265). But normally, even on the Kenai, few carcasses are found in spring. Rather than dying off, overcrowded moose seem to adjust to range limitations by a decrease in calf production, or at least so it would appear on the Kenai. Likewise, willow and birch browse plants are astonishingly durable in the face of even the heaviest overbrowsing. Year after year they continue to sprout after 100 per cent utilization of the previous year's growth. Eventually, however, the sprouts become spindly and finally the plants die. Aspen does not tolerate heavy browsing at all. The effects of overpopulations of moose are by no means as serious as with some other animals, but this is hardly reason for inadequate utilization of the potential crop.

Elsewhere in Alaska, moose ranges appeared to us to be moderately stocked or even understocked, and the present policy of shooting bulls only and attempting to conserve existing breeding stocks is probably entirely justified. Along the Yukon, in fact, more stringent law enforcement, accompanied by a vigorous campaign of conservation education among both natives and whites, will be needed to achieve full stocking.

Predators in relation to moose

Moose are subject to predation by wolves, and some calves likewise are taken by bears.

There is little evidence that the recent peak number of wolves suppressed moose numbers on the better ranges. On the contrary, the spread and increase of moose appears to have occurred concurrently with the rise in wolves. For example, the middle stretches of the Colville River had few or no wolves or moose twenty-five years ago according to the careful account of Smith and Mertie (1930). Moose have increased there rapidly in recent years—even in the past five years we are told by George Gryc of the Geological Survey. So apparently have the wolves, judging from the kill of over 250 by federal workers operating from Umiat last winter. It might be said that the wolves were attracted by and increased with the rising moose population were it not for the fact that most of the wolves were reported to be feeding upon caribou.

Similarly on the Alaska Peninsula, wolves have increased materially according to various old-time residents interviewed by Jay Hammond of the Fish and Wildlife Service. As noted earlier, moose also have increased materially.

There is certainly no inverse correlation between moose and wolf numbers. Hence we wonder about the control of wolves for the protection of moose, particularly when the potential moose crop is not harvested. Along Eagle

River, within 20 miles of Anchorage, we walked a predator control line which was installed to kill wolves and coyotes for the protection of moose and Dall sheep. The area was completely closed to hunting and the moose already were overstocked judging from the "beat up" appearance of the winter range. Predator control when applied as an end in itself, without reference to the existing balance between game and range or to compensatory hunting removal of the surplus, is not necessarily good game management. The same funds might better be spent in more productive channels, such as improvement of winter ranges.

The very low calf crop on the Kenai moose range frequently is charged to predation by black bears, which certainly are abundant. Bears undoubtedly get numerous calves but were the moose population in better balance with the range, we suspect the calf crop would rise irrespective of the bears. Quite by accident a natural experiment has been set up on the Kenai which will permit a test of this hypothesis. A very large fire which burned in 1947 has created a great expanse of new moose winter range which in the next year or so will be invaded by many of the animals that formerly wintered on the badly overbrowsed area near Kenai River. This segment of the population will enjoy for a time almost unrestricted winter forage. Somewhat to the south of the fire are moose that probably will continue to winter on the congested and deteriorating range near Kasilof. If the calf crop in the area of the burn does not materially exceed that of the Kasilof population, the bears can very properly be blamed for the low reproduction. If on the other hand, goodly numbers of calves appear around the burn and a poor crop continues around Kasilof, the problem can be resolved as a function of range. Close observation of this situation will yield valuable leads to guide management, including predator control.

Future study very well may reveal situations where control of predators, as part of a coordinated plan of moose management, will permit a higher yield of moose to hunters. But in our brief tour of the moose ranges we failed to see a single clear-cut example of such integration in management planning. We draw attention again to the unfortunate complications that have arisen on countless deer ranges in the United States when predators and hunting were overregulated without reference to game-range relationships.

Summary

Changes in Alaskan vegetation—some, like fire, caused by man, others climatically controlled—have favored the spread of willow, birch, and aspen, which are critical winter foods of moose. As a result, moose populations generally are increasing, both in the gross area they occupy and in density. Neither predation nor hunting as it is now regulated seem to be critical factors in suppressing moose numbers below what the ranges will support, except around Indian villages along the Yukon where hunting still appears to be limiting.

Elimination of predators and suppression of hunting have created some very heavy moose populations around Cook Inlet; these appear to be damaging their own ranges. The hunting take probably could be much increased in these areas to the benefit of the moose as well as to the hunting public.

In southern and perhaps central Alaska, improvement of moose winter range by controlled burning appears feasible to us. At least experiments along this line would be well worth trying.

As in the case of the caribou, not nearly enough is known about Alaskan moose and moose range to guide future management. Much additional research is needed.

8

THE STATUS OF OTHER
BIG GAME SPECIES

ALASKA is renowned for the richness and variety of its ungulate fauna, there being, besides caribou and moose, four other native species and two introduced species, all of which are of considerable interest. The black-tailed deer of southeastern Alaska is the most numerous of these, followed by the Dall sheep, which occurs on most of the larger mountain ranges, and the mountain goat of the southern mountains. The Arctic prairie once supported a sparse population of muskox and although this interesting animal was exterminated in Alaska at an early date, a small herd has been brought back into the Territory from Greenland and there is a possibility of restoring muskoxen over the northern ranges in the future. Elk and bison, neither native to the Territory, have been imported and naturalized in certain localities. No other area in North America can boast such an array of hoofed game.

In discussing these species we hasten to state that we had comparatively little contact with most of them. Our comments, therefore, reflect only tentative ideas based in part on our own observations and in part on information gener-

ously passed on to us by field men of the Fish and Wildlife
Service and the Wildlife Research Unit at College.

Black-tailed deer

In southeastern Alaska, the black-tailed deer (*Odocoileus
hemionus sitkensis*) is the only widely distributed and
abundant ungulate. It occurs on all the larger islands, as
well as on the mainland (Figure 5), and furnishes considerable hunting over a long season each autumn. At certain times one may enjoy an occasional glimpse of deer
foraging on the beaches. In its principal habitat of dense
undergrowth bordering the heavy Sitka spruce and hemlock
forest, however, the deer is difficult to hunt and difficult
even to see, despite its numbers.

Apparently it is normal for the animals to spend the summer and autumn in the mountains, along the upper edge
of the dense forest, or around openings in the forest itself.
With the first severe weather they migrate down to the
beaches where the winter is spent on a precariously narrow
strip between the tide line and the banked snow under the
forest canopy. Those that survive the winter move back
uphill in spring.

As is so often the case with deer, limitations in the amount
of available winter forage is the bottleneck which checks the
growth of the population. On our boat trip in the region
of Icy Strait we looked over a number of deer winter ranges
with Sigurd Olson, who is studying deer for the Fish and
Wildlife Service. Here and there along the beaches we
found the carcasses of winter-killed deer, nearly all fawns or
old animals with worn teeth, indicating clearly that there are
more deer being produced each year than the winter ranges
will support. Olson was systematically checking sample

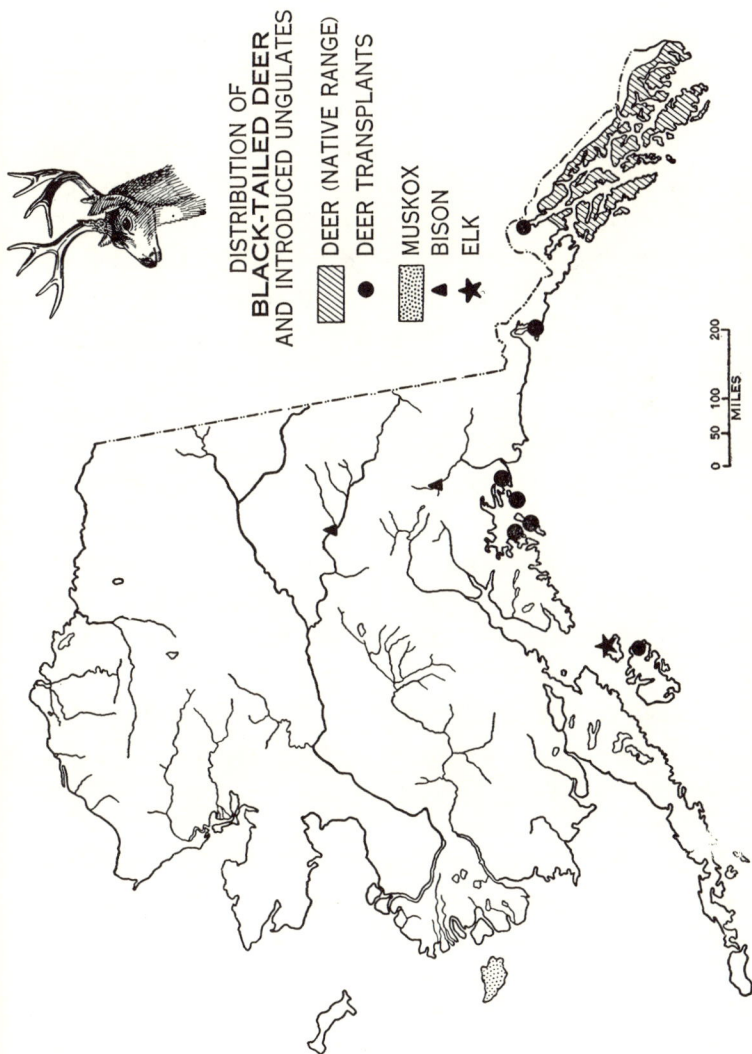

DISTRIBUTION OF
BLACK-TAILED DEER
AND INTRODUCED UNGULATES

DEER (NATIVE RANGE)
DEER TRANSPLANTS
MUSKOX
BISON
ELK

0 50 100 200
MILES

FIGURE 5. Ranges of black-tailed deer, muskox, bison, and elk in Alaska in 1952.

beach lines for dead deer and found 108 fresh carcasses
(from the winter of 1951–52) on an aggregate of 98 miles
of beach. The samples were taken more or less at random
all over southeastern Alaska. Over 80 per cent of the dead
deer were judged to have starved, relatively few being predator or hunter kills. Many older remains were found repre-
senting losses from previous winters. When one considers
that there are at least 12,000 miles of beach line in southeastern Alaska, the magnitude of the winter loss is indicated. One deer lost per mile of beach, along 12,000 beach
line miles, adds up to a staggering annual wastage of animals.

Present hunting regulations permit the killing of bucks
only over a long season (August 20 to November 15) but
with a season limit of two bucks per hunter. During nearly
the whole hunting period the deer are back in the forest
or in the mountains, and it is only in the last week or so
of the season that they come down to the beaches where
they are easily hunted. Most of the kill is taken toward
the end of the season. The aggregate effect of these regulations is a very much circumscribed legal kill. In 1950, for
example, the recorded take by licensed hunters was 2,662
bucks; the estimated take by natives was 2,000, giving a
total harvest of 4,600 deer.

Despite high starvation losses and low legal harvest, the
Territorial government and to a lesser extent the Fish and
Wildlife Service have up to now pursued a policy of rigid
predator control in southeastern Alaska to "protect" the
deer. This situation impresses us as quite parallel to that
of the moose in south-central Alaska, and again we wish to
raise the question of whether deer are really being protected by a program of predator elimination and gross

undershooting. If the real key to deer numbers is the condition of the very poor and submarginal winter range, perhaps the best protection would be *removal of the full annual surplus of deer* to cut down on overbrowsing of critical food plants. Until it is demonstrated that hunters are harvesting the full crop, wolf removal is probably a disservice to the deer, in that it aggravates the natural limitation in range. At best, the available supplies of blueberry, salmonberry, and cedar, which furnish most of the winter browse, are precariously low along the narrow beach lines. In the areas which we visited, there was abundant evidence of overbrowsing, and the bleaching bones of starved deer served mute notice that competition was severe.

Considering the matter from the standpoint of utilization of deer as a resource, it seems clear that a much larger harvest could be permitted, thereby supplying badly needed meat, without in any way endangering the breeding stock of animals. A full harvest would reduce competition on the winter range and greatly reduce winter losses, as practically every state in the northern and western United States has found out. To take a full harvest of deer requires shooting does as well as bucks, which likewise is now common knowledge. In the last year steps have been taken to obtain the facts needed in managing the Alaskan deer herd. Considerable time will be required to translate the research findings into an action program. Perhaps the biggest problem will be convincing the general public that more deer should be killed, when in the recent past a vigorous publicity campaign has urged that more wolves be killed to increase the numbers of deer.

Whereas it seems feasible to improve some winter ranges for moose, we are doubtful of the practicality of doing so for Alaskan deer. The habitable beach lines are so narrow that costs of artificial range management probably would be prohibitive. Yet by way of experiment it might be tried on a limited scale. Release cuttings to stimulate the growth of deer browse could conceivably be worth the cost in selected areas where demand for deer hunting is greatest. The rapidly accelerating program of forest utilization in southeastern Alaska will automatically create much choice summer and autumn range for deer, and where clear-cutting operations are extended to the beach line, some improved winter range may result as well.

In conclusion, the past program of deer management in Alaska, which was premised largely on the supposed need for protecting and building up the breeding stock, appears to us to have fully achieved its purpose. Taking the full harvest of surplus animals now being produced and holding the breeding stock in balance with winter ranges would seem to be the important problems today. The Fish and Wildlife Service is progressing satisfactorily along this new line of approach, but much remains to be done.

Dall sheep and mountain goat

The Dall sheep (*Ovis dalli*), a white counterpart of the western bighorn, is limited in distribution to the mountains of Alaska and a few adjoining ranges in Canada. The mountain goat (*Oreamnos americanus*), actually a close relative of the European chamois, is confined in Alaska to the glacial mountains of the southern coast range, but it occurs widely in western Canada and the northwestern United States. Both of these species, like the caribou, seem to be associated with *climax* vegetation but of a sparse, alpine type rather than the richer tundra and taiga types.

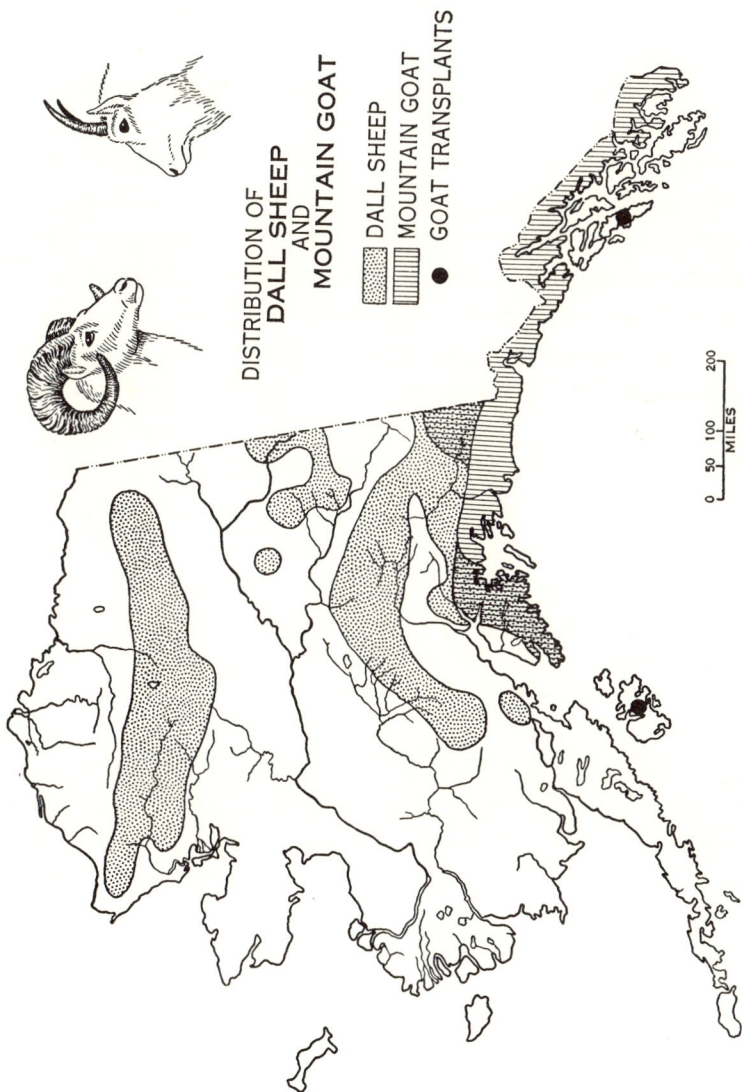

DISTRIBUTION OF
DALL SHEEP
AND
MOUNTAIN GOAT

DALL SHEEP
MOUNTAIN GOAT
● GOAT TRANSPLANTS

0 50 100 200
MILES

FIGURE 6. Ranges of Dall sheep and mountain goat in Alaska in 1952.

Fortunately the arctic-alpine zone in Alaska is subject to little if any disturbance by man, so the habitats of both the sheep and the goat are essentially unaltered, as far as we can see. The ranges of the two species are depicted in Figure 6.

There was considerable evidence of a general decline in numbers of Dall sheep in the period from 1930 to 1945. Murie (1944) and Scott *et al.* (1950) both present data substantiating the decrease, but apparently sheep have been increasing again in recent years. In Mt. McKinley National Park, for example, estimated populations since 1928 are shown in Table 7.

TABLE 7. Estimated populations of Dall sheep in Mt. McKinley National Park in the period 1928 to 1951

Year	Population	Authority
1928	"Peak Numbers"	Murie (1944)
1929–32	"Sharp drop in numbers"	"
1941	1,000–1,500	"
1945	500	Murie (1946)
1947	598	Sumner (1948)
1949	795	Murie (quoted by Scott *et al.*, 1950)
1951	979	Fish and Wildlife Service, R. F. Scott

According to Adolph Murie's observation, the periodic drops in numbers have been attributable primarily to severe winters, which force the sheep to leave their normal haunts in craggy mountains and seek food in foothills and valleys where wolves often add to the already heavy toll. Legal hunting, which is limited to adult rams, probably has little effect on populations today, although local overshooting was common in the past. The kill in the Brooks Range by native peoples seems to be much less than in past years, owing to the fact already mentioned in connection with caribou, that relatively few Eskimos now hunt for a living in the interior. Wolves and coyotes take a good many sheep, but really severe predation probably occurs only under unfavorable winter conditions. Basically, then, weather appears to be the main factor governing year-by-year numbers of sheep, with predation a secondary or corollary influence. Control of the canine predators, at critical times and places, may alleviate the effects of hard winters but there probably will always be weather-caused fluctuations in numbers.

The handsome white rams are among the most esteemed of Alaskan hunting trophies. The total sheep population, estimated by Scott *et al.* (1950) at 12,000, will never contribute heavily to the meat supply of Alaska and should not be thought of as a source of food except very incidentally. The greatest values of the sheep are esthetic and recreational.

Mountain goats are much more circumscribed in range and numbers than sheep, and in general they are more difficult to hunt or even to see. There has been no recorded shrinkage of numbers, although to date the goats have not been studied as intensively as other ungulates in Alaska. No one really knows what factors regulate the level of populations. A successful transplant of mountain goats was made on Baranof Island in 1923, and a similar project is now under way to establish the species on Kodiak Island.

Like the Dall sheep, the mountain goat is valued principally for its interest as part of the mountain fauna. It can never supply a large kill.

Introduced species

We warmly commend the effort of the Fish and Wildlife Service to restore a population of muskox (*Ovibos mo-*

schatus) in Alaska. The original imported animals, brought from Greenland in 1930, were kept for a time in a pen near Fairbanks, but this unsatisfactory arrangement was changed in 1936 when the whole herd, then numbering 31, was moved to Nunivak Island and given complete freedom. Since that date the herd has increased slowly until it now numbers at least 75, which was the number of animals we located in 1952 when flying with David Spencer and Paul Adams.

The low rate of increase in the herd is partly a result of the extremely low breeding potential of the animal, as pointed out by Rouse (1948). However, for a period of years after the animals were brought to Nunivak, the island was severely overgrazed and overbrowsed by excess numbers of reindeer, and no doubt the muskox population suffered from the competition. As mentioned earlier, the willow browse still shows the scars of that period which culminated in a major die-off among the reindeer. Today, with the reindeer herd maintained by the Alaska Native Service at a reasonable level of about 5,000 head, the range for muskox is much improved. Willows, grasses, and sedges which supply most of the winter forage (Rouse, *op. cit.*) are again strong and healthy of growth, and the muskox can reasonably be expected to increase at an accelerated rate.

When an adequate stock is developed on Nunivak Island, it is the hope that reintroductions can be made on the original range of the species, the Arctic slope north of the Brooks Range where the last remnants of native stock were exterminated about eighty-five years ago. Maintenance of a wilderness preserve in the northeastern corner of Alaska, which as stated earlier would serve many scientific and recreational purposes, would also serve to guarantee a permanent habitat for the muskox.

At about the same time the muskoxen were imported from Greenland, a herd of 23 bison (*Bison bison*) was shipped into Alaska from Montana (Dufresne, 1942) and liberated on an area of grassy alluvium near Big Delta, along the Tanana River. A substantial population has built up, permitting a limited kill of 25 bulls a year for the last three years. In 1950, 17 head from Big Delta were moved to a more or less similar habitat along the Copper River where a new nucleus seems to be becoming established. Although the bison experiment may be judged successful to date, there are very few other sites in Alaska where the animals can be put, and it is most unlikely that any material expansion of the population either can be or should be attempted. Even now grass is being replaced by brush at Big Delta, perhaps because of the grazing of bison.

Elk (*Cervus canadensis*) from the State of Washington were imported in the period 1926–29 and liberated on Afognak, Revilla, and Kruzof islands. Only the animals on Afognak have persisted. In 1938 the population was recorded as 212. The 1952 elk count was 345. In 1950, and again in 1952, a limited number of permits were issued for killing bulls. The elk, like the bison, appears to be adapted to only a few situations in the Territory. Money and effort spent in managing these exotic forms might better be devoted to improving management of the infinitely more important native ungulates.

Summary

The black-tailed deer, along with the caribou and moose, must be considered a major big game species, capable of furnishing a large amount of hunting and recreation, and a high yield of meat. The other ungulates in Alaska are of less over-all importance. Some have high esthetic values, and some can furnish additional trophy hunting and limited amounts of meat. Both research and management budgets should consider these relative values in allocating funds.

9

A BROAD APPROACH
TO MANAGEMENT

A REGIONAL ECONOMY is molded by two ele-
ments—first, the quantity and availability of resources derived from the earth or adjoining sea, and second, by the
skill and intensity with which these products are extracted,
processed, or utilized by man.

It is axiomatic that a region poor in resources lacks the
capacity to support the wealthy and complex economy of
better endowed areas, however clever and determined the
inhabitants may be. But it is equally true that all land
has values and the human ecologist seeks to define the
highest use to which each acre, rich or poor, may be put
best to serve society. Graham (1944:98) has reduced this
principle to a formula.

By Graham's standards, or any others, Alaska is predominantly a barren and unproductive region in terms of
its capacity to support agriculture, industry, or high taxes.
Such exploitable resources as exist (principally fish, timber,
and water power, mostly in the south) should indeed be
utilized to the utmost, with due provision for sustained
yield, but the bulk of the Territory offers little hope of
"development" in the ordinary chamber-of-commerce sense

of the word. It is Class VII and Class VIII land, suitable locally for light grazing (as by reindeer) or logging, but mostly useful for wildlife and recreation. To tear up the wilderness in such a country, hoping to produce something "better," is often a serious mistake. In our judgment the values which already exist on much of the Territory—wild fish and game, and the opportunity for wilderness recreation —offer the highest use to which the land can be put. How to make the most of these assets, particularly of big game, is the subject of our essay.

The importance of the range

In the fifty years that have elapsed since the conservation movement was born in North America, we have learned much about the basic forces that regulate populations of wild animals. Perhaps the most significant advance is our understanding of the supreme importance of *habitat* as a population control. Over and over, with countless species in many lands, it has been demonstrated that land use, as it affects game habitat, is the primary determinant of game abundance or scarcity. Here in Alaska our brief survey again appears to support this thesis. The shrinkage of the caribou herds, the rise and crash of the reindeer, the spread and increase of moose, all seem to stem from habitat changes that have occurred since the advent of white domination in Alaska. Furthermore, the future trends of these populations can almost surely be regulated by deliberately controlling two of the principal influences on range conditions—fire, and numbers of grazing animals.

In our opinion this approach to the management of big game animals in Alaska should receive more attention than it has in the past. In both the programs of the Fish and

Wildlife Service, dealing with wild species, and of the Alaska Native Service, dealing with the semidomesticated reindeer, there is still undue emphasis on controlling the kill and not enough emphasis on understanding and managing the range. Whereas in the recent past, protection of breeding stocks *was* the main problem, that is not universally so today. The budget and administrative program of the Fish and Wildlife Service is still designed to cope largely with the direct decimating factors—hunting and predation—the main objective being to increase breeding stocks of the big game herds, rather than to increase yields. In building up stocks (and fine progress can be reported in this direction) inadequate reference is made to range capacities or limitations. Some areas, such as moose ranges near Cook Inlet and deer ranges in the southeast, are clearly stocked to capacity already and some of the potential yield is being wasted. Underharvest of big game animals is often a more serious mistake than overharvest, because of repercussions on the range. But this danger is not being adequately considered nor fully investigated.

It is not enough to blame the uninformed public or the game commission for the continuance of outmoded policies of managing big game. The Fish and Wildlife Service should be gathering the basic facts needed for managing big game species and using those facts to mold public opinion. We are happy indeed to note that a beginning is being made in this direction, but much more stress should be added.

The reindeer program of the Alaska Native Service appears to us likewise to be emphasizing minor considerations rather than the transcendent question of range condition. Problems of ownership of the deer, herding and care, slaughter and distribution, are being well attended, but only one man, hired in 1952, is studying the range on which regrowth of the whole industry will be dependent, and he is burdened with many administrative duties. The service desperately needs a technical range crew whose recommendations should guide all other phases of reindeer management.

We hasten to add that the present programs of both of the above bureaus have many admirable and sound features, as well as competent personnel. Both are struggling against difficult odds, such as budget limitations, transportation difficulties, and outside pressures. Such practical considerations often limit what an organization can do, but they should not be permitted to dictate the formulation of policy—of what the agency is *trying* to do. Our criticism is directed at the inadequacy of present policy. Conservation of the range should be dominant over conservation of the individual animal, not the other way around.

Coordination in government programs

If well managed and fully utilized, the big game herds of Alaska can be a continuing resource of great value to the Territory. Caribou, moose, and reindeer could supply a considerable proportion of the meat required by Alaskans, both white and native (though not military establishments), and at the same time offer recreational hunting. The opportunity to see the large ungulates, and for a few to shoot them, will augment the flow of tourists and of tourist dollars. There is the chance in Alaska to make game management a primary industry rather than an adjunct or "orphan sister" of more intensive forms of land use, as is the case in so much of the United States.

But this high objective can be achieved only if game administration is planned on a broad base in which the land and its vegetation—the game habitat—is the major consideration. Such an approach will require coordinated action by a number of government bureaus.

There is for example the matter of fire and its control. At the moment, over most of Alaska, wildfire is almost exclusively the worry of the Bureau of Land Management. It should be very much the worry of the Fish and Wildlife Service and of the Alaska Native Service since it is a major influence on the ranges of caribou, moose, and locally of reindeer. A comprehensive fire control program should recognize primary game ranges as well as primary silvicultural sites, and a system of priorities might be drawn to concentrate protection on the most valuable and critical spots. On a few of the best moose ranges in the south, controlled burning might enter the picture, though obviously the acreage to be so intensively managed will never be large. In the southeast, the Forest Service is primarily concerned with fire, but again where there are effects on fish, bears, deer, and other wildlife, the Fish and Wildlife Service has more than a passing interest. On national parks and monuments the Park Service likewise is involved. Primary recreation areas (camp sites, etc.) are of concern to several bureaus. They certainly require special protection.

A problem of such wide scope needs coordinated, inter-bureau planning. Perhaps the Alaska Field Committee, appointed by the Secretary of Interior for just such purpose, can catalyze a comprehensive fire control program.

Another problem requiring coordinated action is the matter of conservation education. Enforcement of the game laws, control of fire, keeping camp sites clean, and preserving park and wilderness areas are all dependent upon support and understanding on the part of Alaskan residents (white and native alike), visiting tourists, and temporary military personnel. The several bureaus and the two school systems, native and territorial, could well work closely together on a unified program rather than each dabbling independently in the conservation education field.

In these and many other ways, game administration can be incorporated as an integral part in the guided development of Alaska. Without such incorporation, the full potential of wildlife can never be realized.

The challenge of conservation in Alaska

At the outset we stated that ideally a program of conservation and of land use should be devised before a new country is developed. Unfortunately the motive for conservation usually is impending shortage, which leads us to trim the resource boat after it is half full of water. But in Alaska, despite some buffeting about, the land resources are still largely intact, and what is more, they are still in government rather than private hands. The problem of planning and executing the best possible development of the Territory is therefore squarely up to the government. The fact that resources are limited rather than rich and abundant is no disadvantage. On the contrary, this situation reduces economic pressure and facilitates centralized management.

There is need for much more research on the technological aspects of conservation. There must be more coordination between the various branches than has been the case in the past, and much better application of the ecologic principles of land management. We have attempted to examine merely one small facet of the problem, but even our limited approach demonstrates the need for broader planning. Others qualified to explore parallel problems, such as the future development of the fisheries, or of tourist trade, or of forest industries would doubtless find parallel shortcomings. But if these mechanical and administrative difficulties can be overcome, we visualize an unusual opportunity for application of the principles of conservation to a fascinating and magnificent stretch of country.

BIBLIOGRAPHY

Aaltonen, V. T.
1919 Kangasmetsein luonnollisesta üüdestumisesta Soumen Lapessa, I. *Communicationes ex instituto quaestionum forestalium finlandiae*, 1:1–319 (German summary, pp. 1–56).

Alaska Field Committee, U.S. Dept. of Interior.
1951 A six-year integrated program, Department of the Interior in Alaska, 1952–1957 (K. J. Kadow, Chairman).
1952 Department of the Interior program for Alaska, 1954–1959 (George W. Rogers, Chairman), 162 pp. mimeo.

Anderson, R. M.
1924 Range of the moose extending northward. *Can. Field-Nat.*, 38:27–29.

Banfield, A. W. F.
1951 The barren-ground caribou. Canada Dept. Resources and Development, Ottawa, 56 pp. mimeo.

Burdick, C. G.
1940 Report to the Secretary of the Interior, Reindeer Acquisition Unit, F.Y., Alaska Native Service, Juneau, 33 pp. mimeo.

Culver, W. G.
1923 Report of moose on Kenai Peninsula. U.S. Fish and Wildlife Service, Juneau, 7 pp. mimeo.

Dufresne, F.
1942 Mammals and birds of Alaska. *U.S.D.I. Fish and Wildlife Service Circ.* 3, 37 pp.
1946 *Alaska's animals and fishes.* A. S. Barnes and Co., N.Y., 297 pp.

Graham, E. H.
1944 *Natural principles of land use.* Oxford Univ. Press, N.Y., 274 pp.

GREEN, D. D.
1950 Predator control problems in Alaska. Paper delivered to First Alaska Science Conference, Washington, D.C. (U.S. Fish and Wildlife Service, Washington, D.C.), 13 pp. mimeo.

HADWEN, S.
1939 A visit to the Mackenzie River delta. *Ontario Res. Found. Bull.*, 6(12).

HANSON, H. C.
1952 Importance and development of the reindeer industry in Alaska. *Journ. Range Management*, 5:243–51.

HUSTICH, I.
1951 The lichen woodlands in Labrador and their importance as winter pastures for domesticated reindeer. *Acta Geographica*, 12:1–48.

KALELA, O.
1948 Metsakäuriin esiintymisestä Soumessa ja sen levinneisyyden muutoksista lähialueilla (The occurrence of roe deer in Finland and changes in its distribution in the adjoining areas). *Soumen Riista*, 3:34–56.
1949 Changes in geographic ranges in the avifauna of northern and central Europe in relation to recent changes in climate. *Bird Banding*, 20:77–103.

LANTIS, M.
1950 The reindeer industry in Alaska. *Arctic*, 3:27–44.

LEFFINGWELL, E. DE K.
1919 The Canning River region, northern Alaska. *U.S.G.S. Prof. Paper* 109, 251 pp.

LEOPOLD, A. S.
1950 Deer in relation to plant succession. *Trans. North Amer. Wildlife Conf.*, 15:571–78.

LUTZ, H. J.
1950 Ecological effects of forest fires in the interior of Alaska. Paper delivered to First Alaska Science Conterence, Washington, D.C. (Yale School of Forestry, New Haven, Conn.), 9 pp. mimeo.

LYNGE, B.
1921 Studies on the lichen flora of Norway. Skrifter utgit av videnshapsselskapet i Kristiania, 1921. *Matematisk-Naturvidenskabelig Klasse*, 1, Bd. 7, 252 pp.

MERTIE, J. B., JR.

1930 The Chandalar-Sheenjek district, Alaska. In *Mineral resources of Alaska, 1927, U.S.G.S. Bull.* 810, pp. 87–139.

MURIE, A.

1944 The wolves of Mount McKinley. *Fauna U.S. Nat'l Parks No.* 5, 238 pp.

1946 Another look at McKinley Park sheep. *Living Wilderness,* December, 1946, pp. 1–3.

MURIE, O. J.

1935 Alaska-Yukon caribou. *North Amer. Fauna No.* 54, 93 pp.

OSGOOD, W. H.

1901 Natural history of the Cook Inlet region, Alaska. *North Amer. Fauna No.* 21, pp. 51–87.

PALMER, L. J.

1940 Caribou versus fire in interior Alaska. Unpubl. MS., 5 pp. typewritten (copy on file Alaska Cooperative Wildlife Research Unit, College).

1941 Caribou versus fire in interior Alaska: A study of burned-over lichen ranges. Unpubl. MS., 14 pp. typewritten (copy on file Alaska Cooperative Wildlife Research Unit, College).

1945 The Alaska tundra and its use by reindeer. U.S.D.I., Office of Indian Affairs, Washington, D.C., 28 pp. mimeo.

PETERSON, R. L.

1952 Älgen, Studier, jakt och vård. By Folke Skuncke [Review of]. *Journ. Wildlife Mngt.,* 16:218–19.

PRESNALL, C.

1950 The predation question—facts versus fancies. *Trans. North Amer. Wildlife Conf.,* 15:197–207.

RAUSCH, R.

1951 Notes on the Nunamiut Eskimo and mammals of the Anaktuvuk Pass region, Brooks Range, Alaska. *Arctic,* 4:147–95.

ROBERTS, B.

1942 The reindeer industry in Alaska. *Polar Record,* 3:568–72.

ROUSE, C. H.

1948 Muskoxen on Nunivak Island. U.S. Fish and Wildlife Service, Juneau, 9 pp. mimeo.

Rowell, L.-G.
    1922 Hänglavar och tillvaxt hos norrländsk grass. (Bartflechten
        und Zuwachs bei der norrländischen Fichte) *Med-
        delanden från Statens Skogsförsöksanstalt*, 19:405–51.
Scheffer, V. B.
    1951 The rise and fall of a reindeer herd. *Scientific Monthly*,
        73:356–62.
Schrader, F. C.
    1900 Preliminary report on a reconnaissance along the Chan-
        dalar and Koyukuk Rivers in Alaska in 1899. *U.S.G.S.
        Twenty-first Ann. Rep.*, pt. 2, pp. 441–86.
    1904 A reconnaissance in northern Alaska. *U.S.G.S. Prof.
        Paper 20*, 139 pp.
Schwatka, F.
    1885 *Along Alaska's great river.* Cassell and Co., Ltd., N.Y.,
        360 pp.
Scott, R. F.
    1951 Wildlife in the economy of Alaska natives. *Trans. North
        Amer. Wildlife Conf.*, 16:508–23.
Scott, R. F., Chatelain, E. F., and Elkins, W. A.
    1950 The status of the Dall sheep and caribou in Alaska.
        Trans. North Amer. Wildlife Conf., 15:612–25.
Shuman, R. F.
    1950 Bear depredations on red salmon spawning populations
        in the Karluk River system, 1947. *Jour. Wildlife
        Mngt.*, 14:1–9.
Siivonen, L.
    1952 On the influence of climatic variations of recent decades
        on game economy. *Fennia*, 75:77–88.
Skuncke, F.
    1949 *Älgen, Studier, jakt och vård.* P. A. Norstedt and Soners,
        Stockholm, Sweden. 400 pp.
Smith, P. S., and Mertie, J. B., Jr.
    1930 Geology and mineral resources of northwestern Alaska.
        U.S.G.S. Bull. 815, 351 pp.
Spencer, D. L., Nelson, U. C., and Elkins, W. A.
    1951 America's greatest goose-brant nesting area. *Trans. North
        Amer. Wildlife Conf.*, 16:290–95.
Stanton, W. J.
    1953 Economic aspects of recreation in Alaska. *Alaska Recrea-*

tion Survey, U.S. National Park Service, pt. 1, vol. 1, 191 pp.

STEFANSSON, V.

1913 *My life with the Eskimo.* Macmillan Co., N.Y., 527 pp.

SUMNER, L.

1948 An air census of Dall sheep in Mount McKinley National Park. *Journ. Wildlife Mngt.*, 12:302–4.

U.S. DEPT. OF AGRICULTURE

1949 Report on exploratory investigation of agricultural problems of Alaska. *Agric. Res. Admin., Misc. Publ. No. 700*, Washington, D.C.

U.S. DEPT. OF INTERIOR

1951 The Pribilof report, 1949: Living conditions among the natives of the Pribilof Islands and other communities of the Bering Sea area. U.S.D.I., Washington, D.C., 81 pp.

INDEX